Get a Financial Life

Your money in your twenties

Get a Financial Life

Your money in your twenties

Nic Cicutti

A & C Black • London

First published in the United Kingdom in 2009 by

A & C Black Publishers Ltd
36 Soho Square, London W1D 3QY
www.acblack.com

A CIP record for this book is available from the British Library.

ISBN: 9-781-4081-0115-5

This book is produced using paper that is made from wood grown in managed, sustainable forests. It is natural, renewable and recyclable. The logging and manufacturing processes conform to the environmental regulations of the country of origin.

Design by Fiona Pike, Pike Design, Winchester
Typeset by RefineCatch Ltd, Bungay, Suffolk
Printed in the United Kingdom by CPI Bookmarque, Croydon

Contents

CONTENTS

Acknowledgements

One thing you learn when writing a book is that it really is a collaborative effort.

So I suppose the first person to blame for what you now hold in your hands is Sarah Pennells, who suggested me as its possible author to the publishers, A & C Black. Then there's Lisa Carden, who was brave enough to commission me. Camilla Garton and Kate Stenner picked through my wordy prose, grammatical errors and stylistic *non sequiturs*. My apologies to them all.

When I started out as a journalist, I was taught always to have a firm picture in your head of who you are aiming your copy at. For me, that person is my nephew Ben, university student and perennially deluded West Ham fan, whom I rate as a special friend – along with his brother Dominic. Cheers, lads.

A special thanks goes to Ann Fannin and Joyce Woods, who offered friendship and sympathy during the writing process. Thanks also to Sally, our rough collie, who looked on dolefully as I swore at the computer screen.

My most important debt of gratitude goes to my partner Tina Cambell. She has always offered me love and support during our journey together. I dedicate this book to Tina, with all of my own – often inadequate but everlasting – love.

Introduction

Every year, more than 300,000 graduates in their early 20s leave university, armed with a degree and a determination to lead successful lives – although how that 'success' is measured ultimately depends, as always, on the individual concerned.

As one of these recent graduates, the new world you are entering is vastly different to the one you have just left. Whereas until now it was perfectly possible to muddle through, safe in the knowledge that whatever happened – good or bad – it was only a temporary phase in your life, the minute you leave college everything changes.

In the 'real' world, you will face a completely new set of pressures. The first and most obvious is that without money it is very difficult to survive easily. You will be expected to find a proper job, to get to it on time every day, to live in relatively decent accommodation, to pay for things without constantly having to borrow money off your parents or your bank.

Of course, none of this is obligatory. At the end of the day you are free to live your life how you want. But most people in their 20s broadly feel that these new 'rules' governing the way they are now expected to lead their lives are acceptable, at least in general if not in every specific detail.

Either way, another of the big discoveries made by many people in their 20s is that money is neither easy to make nor to keep hold of.

There are hundreds of temptations out there, decisions to be made or avoided, all of which involve the potential for huge errors. Of course, there's nothing wrong with making mistakes: if we didn't make them, we would be much poorer for it in lots of ways.

But some of those mistakes, particularly the financial ones, can have pretty devastating long-term consequences. Moreover, if there is one thing that marks out today's generation of 20-somethings, it is that the world they are entering is immeasurably less hospitable than it has been for decades.

Finding a job is much more difficult than it used to be, while credit – essential to many graduates for the first few years of their working lives – is now much harder to obtain and more expensive for those lucky enough to be offered it. Getting through your 20s is probably more of a challenge than it was for your parents, certainly on the money side of things.

Every penny counts, therefore: spending what you have carefully and saving what you can spare more effectively matters more today than it has ever done.

This book aims to help you do that. Like any other book on finance, this is most definitely NOT meant to be something you read through in one go. What it tries to do, in fairly shorthand format, is address many of the key issues you are likely to face in the first few years after leaving college. If and when they do crop up, it will hopefully provide some pointers as to what you can do next, or mistakes you may want to avoid.

None of what's in here, however, is a substitute for your own decision-making abilities. All of us have those skills within ourselves; apart from anything else, they are often simply an extension of basic common sense.

What this book tries to do is marry that common sense with some additional information and tips you may need. Hopefully it will save you more money than its purchase price over the course of the next few years.

Financial websites and consumer forums

You will find many relevant and useful websites mentioned in each chapter. One of the fantastic things about the Internet is that it allows for discussion, debate and advice to be exchanged.

If you know your way around the Internet even just a little, you will almost certainly have come across the websites of the main newspaper groups in the UK. All of them carry content from their own personal finance sections. In some cases, they carry additional online content too.

Debate and in-depth sharing of information is a cornerstone to the ability to make good financial decisions. Several excellent websites allow you to do that. They include:

Money Saving Expert: www.moneysavingexpert.com

Interactive Investor: www.iii.co.uk

Motley Fool: www.fool.co.uk

Which?: www.which.co.uk

All facts and figures were correct at time of going to press.

Life PART I

1
Money and work

Finding work

Every year, more than 300,000 new graduates hit the jobs market, joining thousands more who may have spent a few years with their first employer but are now looking for a fresh challenge.

Unfortunately, if ever there were a 'wrong' time to be looking for work, today is it. The financial crisis that has engulfed not only the UK but all Western economies since late 2007 has made life immeasurably more difficult for many new graduates.

Unemployment has grown sharply in the past 12 months and many experts believe it is likely to rise to more than 3 million. In January 2009, a study from High Fliers Research, a market research firm, found recruitment targets among the 100 top UK companies had been cut by 17 per cent.

What that means in practice is that if you harboured any dreams of a swift and easy transition from penniless undergraduate to well-paid high flier, you can forget them right now. For the next 18 months or so – at the very least – the road ahead will be far rockier than you ever could have thought when going to college was little more than a glimmer in your imagination four or five years ago.

So how can you minimise the chances of being in such a position yourself? The first thing to realise is that not every employer has cut back on jobs in the past year or so. Even where they have, the cutbacks are neither universal in their scope, nor permanent. In every recession, some firms do better than others, or they pull through more quickly.

Nor are the jobs that are available 'bad': they will simply be different from the ones you originally may have envisaged for yourself. The trick is to know who to target for a job and when – and making sure that when you do, your application stands out from all the others.

So how do you go about bagging a job and keeping it – and, when you are ready, moving on to the next one?

This book can't supply all the ins and outs of how to apply for a job successfully. There are plenty of excellent websites and books to help you do that, not least Martin Yate's *Great Answers to Tough Interview Questions* (Kogan Page), and two books in the Steps to Success series: *Get that Job: CVs* and *Get that Job: Interviews*.

However, here are a few words of advice.

There are likely to be four key phases to getting the job you want:

- researching the job
- preparing a CV
- writing a covering letter
- attending an interview

But before you even begin the process of applying, there is one vital thing you need to be: *confident*.

A survey by the *Guardian* newspaper and the recruitment agency Barkers found that 'positive thinking', 'proactivity' and 'decisiveness' differentiate those who are successful (defined by the researchers as those who find a job within four months) from the rest.

So, now that you are geed up and optimistic, this is what you need to do.

Research the job

What information should you be looking for?

The kind of things you need to have a strong understanding of are:

- what the company does and the sector it operates in;
- its structure (annual turnover and profits, number of employees, geographical distribution, key divisions and senior executives);
- its history and corporate ethos;
- its key rivals, if any – what they do, how they go about it, their strong and weak points.

Create a superb CV

Here are four key tips to help you do that.

- **Keep it brief.** Enough said.
- **Don't lie.** Don't ever make up experiences or qualifications or that you can't substantiate. You will be caught out.
- **Show them you are human. Don't try to be clever.** Unusual fonts, wacky layouts, funny pictures will count against you.
- **Avoid spelling mistakes.** Many employers chuck CVs with spelling mistakes straight in the bin. It once happened to me.

Write a blinding covering letter

By definition, first impressions count. Here are some useful tips to follow when preparing your letter.

- **Always find out who you are writing to.** Avoid writing 'Dear Sir/Madam'.
- **Get it right.** And give your contact details.
- **Be brief.** You don't need more than a few paragraphs to say why you are applying for this job.
- **Think about your email.** Make sure all your key points are at the top, avoiding the need to scroll down the page.
- **Always ask for an interview.** Be confident without sounding arrogant.

Do a fantastic interview

Here is what you should do and say on the day.

- Be there in plenty of time.
- Look clean and tidy.
- Avoid heavy perfumes or aftershave – and don't smoke, even if you are nervous.
- Be a good actor. Smile and nod in the right places.
- Don't rabbit on.
- Never slag off your old bosses or your previous job, even if they were horrible.
- Show you've researched the company and your proposed job thoroughly.
- Make sure you have well-thought-out answers to some typical questions you are likely to be asked.
- Go armed with a few questions of your own.

Work, money and tax

Let's be honest, very few of us work purely for the fun of it.

You may not feel able to ask all the probing questions you might want to at the interview stage, but there are always employment-related money issues to consider when thinking about taking a job. Lack of space means they can't all be discussed in this book, but here are a few things worth bearing in mind.

Income tax and National Insurance

At the end of the day, if the government wants to spend money on schools, education, the UK's transport infrastructure etc, it needs our money.

The way it gets this money is by HM Revenue & Customs collecting a range of taxes from us. Each year the Chancellor sets out how much it costs to provide all these services and how much tax is needed to pay for them.

The calculations

Among other things, you pay income tax on:

- your wages
- your business profits if you are self-employed
- some benefits, like jobseeker's allowance and incapacity benefit

As well as paying income tax on your wages or income from self-employment, you also have to pay National Insurance contributions (NICs).

If you are an employee, your employer operates PAYE (pay as you earn) and deducts tax and NICs from your wages. If you are self-employed, you are responsible for paying your own tax and NICs and filling in an annual self assessment tax form.

How much tax should you be paying?

Working this out is simple. This is because there are three tax bands, plus an annual allowance on which no tax is paid. These figures are for the 2009–10 financial year:

- if you earn between £0 and £6,475, no tax is paid;
- on the next £37,400, tax is levied at 20 per cent;
- thereafter, tax is payable at 40 per cent.

All you need to do is work out how much of your earnings fall into each tax band and deduct the appropriate percentage from each slice – without forgetting your original allowance. Simple, isn't it?

Of course, you then need to work out your National Insurance contributions. In the 2009–10 tax year, they are:

National Insurance for employees

- If you earn above £110 a week (the 'earnings threshold') and up to £844 per week, you pay 11 per cent of this amount as so-called 'Class 1' NICs.

- You also pay 1 per cent of earnings above £844 a week as Class 1 NICs.
- You pay a lower amount of NICs as an employee if you are a member of your employer's contracted-out pension scheme. Essentially, this means you receive a rebate of NI contributions in return for a smaller state second pension. You should ask your human resources or wages department about this.

Self-employed

If you are self-employed, you pay two separate types of NICs. They include so-called Class 2 NICs at a flat rate weekly amount of £2.40 in the 2009–10 tax year.

You also pay Class 4 NICs as a percentage of your taxable profits – you pay 8 per cent on annual taxable profits between £5,715 and £43,875 and 1 per cent on any taxable profit over that amount.

Your tax code

When you start working, you receive a number allocated to you on the basis of your earnings, your employment status and family responsibilities. This number basically reflects how much tax is taken from you.

While it is easy to work out how much tax you should pay based on the calculations above, potential deductions are determined by a range of additional factors. This is why it can be useful to check your tax code too. Directgov, the Government's information website, has some excellent information on how your tax code is calculated. If you have any queries, you can also raise them with your local tax office: it may sound hard to believe, but tax office staff are usually amazingly helpful and friendly.

Income tax on savings and investments

You pay income tax on the income you get from your savings and investments. This includes:

- bank and building society interest
- dividends from shares
- rents from any investment properties you own

Bank and building society interest and dividends are usually 'taxed at source', which means tax is deducted before the interest is paid to you.

The way tax is levied on savings is confusingly different to what you pay on your work-related income. This is largely because, although the government scrapped the 10p starting tax rate for earned income, it has not done so for other income.

Basically, for the financial year 2009–10, it works like this:

- the first £2,440 of savings income is taxed at 10 per cent – although in practice any tax payable is almost certain to be above this limit, as the interest is added to your other income;
- savings income that rises above £2,440 but under £37,400 is taxable at 20 per cent. Earnings above that level are taxed at 40 per cent.

If you're a non-taxpayer, you may be able to claim some tax back. If you're a higher rate taxpayer, you'll have more tax to pay. See the HMRC website (www.hmrc.gov.uk) for more information.

Other taxes

Most of this subject is outside the scope of a book which really aims at helping people in their mid-20s to deal with their finances. After all, the chances are you will only be called to deal with them later on in life, perhaps in your 30s and 40s. That said, there are still some things that you may need to know, if only to provide you with a starting point for a more detailed look at the issues at some future stage.

Inheritance tax (IHT)

IHT affects people in different ways. For most of our lives, it is something we pay if relatives or family were to die and leave us some money or another asset – jewellery, a home or similar. Then, when we become old ourselves, it turns into something we start to think about, as we prepare to leave assets to our own kids and grandkids.

For the sake of this book, I am going to treat IHT from the point of view of the inheritor, which is far more likely to be your situation at this stage in your life.

So how much tax is payable and on what? Depending on how much money is involved overall, the 'estate' of the deceased person will be liable to pay tax on any assets over £325,000 in 2009 – 10. The rate of tax at which IHT is payable is currently 40 per cent.

So if you are left a house worth £500,000, the first £325,000 is not taxed and you pay 40 per cent tax on the remaining £175,000 – a total of £70,000.

The way those assets are calculated is that on the death of a person, their estate undergoes a process called probate, which involves approval by a court and some legal expense.

Put simply, solicitors and the executor of that dead person's will tot up what the estate owns after all bills have been paid and present these accounts to the tax authorities. If there is a tax bill to pay, the money is handed over and you – and any other beneficiaries – divide the rest, as set out in the will.

The important point to note here is that although the government receives £2.5bn in IHT a year, a lot of that would not need to be paid if those affected had planned against it. The reality is that there are plenty of ways to cut an IHT bill. Although for most 20-somethings this is not really an area worth thinking about yet, if you do have significant assets, you should definitely talk to a tax expert.

Capital gains tax (CGT)
This is another tax which is unlikely to affect you right now. But it is still worth knowing a little about it.

At its simplest, CGT is payable if you sell something for more than you paid for it. Shares, land, buildings, part of a business and expensive antiques or jewellery are the sorts of things that will usually attract a CGT liability. However, you may also have to pay CGT if you simply give something away or receive compensation or prize money.

On the other hand, you do not have to pay CGT if you are selling or otherwise passing on personal belongings that are worth less than £6,000, or if you give assets to a registered charity. Nor is it payable when selling your private car and your main home, or when you receive money from ISAs, premium bonds, betting, lottery or pools winnings, or personal injury compensation.

You do not have to pay tax on gains below £9,600 (in the 2009–10 tax year). Above that, the rate of tax payable is 18 per cent.

As with inheritance tax, there are many ways of reducing the tax bill further. If you ever find yourself owning assets like that and need to work out ways of cutting the CGT bill, talk to an expert.

Moving on

It is quite possible that after a couple of years in the same job, you may want to look for fresh challenges.

Many of the points discussed above are 100 per cent relevant to your new job, certainly in terms of the specifics involved in applying for it.

But there is more to it than that, of course. For many people, there is a process involved in the decision to change employers, with lots of issues that need to be resolved.

Here are some questions that you might want to ask yourself in terms of why you want to move and the next job you are moving to:

- is it about money and promotion? This raises issues about whether you are stuck in a rut, are unhappy with the workplace or the type of work itself.
- what do you actually like doing? Hopefully, your current job will have given you some indications as to what you like and dislike and where you want to go next.
- are you up for a new challenge and do you have the skills? With some people, there is a distinct lack of realism. They risk rejection through lack of professional preparation.

What next?

If you have sat down and worked out that you really do want to seek out fresh challenges, here are some tips worth considering:

1   investigate where you want to go. Talk to others in the area of work you are considering. Look at the pros and cons in detail: hours, salary, organisational culture.

2   if the job requires re-training, find out exactly what – and how you will survive in the meantime.

3   see if there are stepping stones to get there. For example, volunteering or a week's experience may help you decide whether to take it further.

4   use your existing job to boost your experiences more widely. Seize every chance to improve your skills. Go on training courses if they are available.

5   think laterally. The job you want may well be one you've never considered. And the skills you have may not always be ones your future employers considered worth having. You may be able to persuade them differently.

6   be careful. Lots of people make unsuitable applications, especially if they are unhappy in their existing jobs. Be sure that isn't you.

7   tell friends and family that you are job-hunting – being asked how it's going will keep you motivated. It also raises the possibility of them tipping you off about a suitable vacancy.

similarly, contact people you meet at conferences and even your old alumni/college networks. If you know someone who works for an employer that sounds interesting, ask them to recommend you.

Finally, give it time. Most people find that from the moment they are unhappy in their old job to the point at which they get a new one can take up to six months. Good luck!

Contacts and links

Prospects: there are plenty of websites offering great material to graduates starting out. Prospects is the UK's official careers website and has loads of useful tools you may want to look at. Go to www.prospects.ac.uk.

Money and leisure

It may seem weird to be talking about leisure in the same context as work. The reality, however, is that you can't decide what to do about work without examining why you even want to bother working or how hard.

For almost 20 years, people have tended to work harder and harder. In January 2009, a survey by the Trades Union Congress revealed that in the previous year employers benefited from record levels of unpaid overtime provided by their workers.

The TUC, whose figures were based on analysis of official statistics, found that more than five million people gave free overtime worth £26.9bn by staying at work longer than their contracted hours – the highest number since records began in 1992.

The average amount was seven hours and six minutes a week, worth an extra £5,139 a year to workers – had they had been properly paid for all this extra work. The previous record was in 2001, when five million employees worked unpaid overtime.

The statistics covered hours worked in the 12 months to mid-2008, before the economic recession took hold. As workers feel increasingly insecure about their jobs in the current recession, the trend towards more unpaid overtime is likely to increase.

In some ways, the trend towards working harder is actually quite surprising. Until recently, real incomes had been rising for people in work over many years. Given this fact, you would expect people with rising living standards to spend fewer hours at work and use their increased earning power to enjoy more leisure time. Yet that does not seem to happen.

How do we know when we have the right balance between earning money and enjoying leisure time? These are five ideas that may help.

1 Decide the income you need

At the end of the day, money is a means to an end, not an end in itself. So what income would allow you to pay your bills and set aside a certain amount for the future? Remember: if all your time is spent earning money, when will you ever be able to spend it in a way you can genuinely enjoy?

2 Decide how much your leisure time is worth

Many people focus solely on the amount they are earning. But life is never that simple: if you earn another £100 by working on a Saturday or late in the evening, the reality is that you will only be taking home £50 or £60 of that after tax and travel bills. Is it worth giving up your leisure time, and forfeiting relationships with friends, for that extra money? There are times when that level of leisure sacrifice may be necessary – but if so, make it a finite period, not an open-ended one.

3 Beware of the law of diminishing returns

If you earn £40,000 by working a 45-hour week, how much better off will you feel because you have earned £55,000 – but sacrificed another 10 hours of your free time between Monday and Friday? Bear in mind that once you have taken a typical eight hours' sleep each day, plus three hours' travel, shopping and eating, those extra 10 hours are worth 50 per cent of your leisure time each day.

4 Don't become a workaholic

Some people get into the habit of working hard. They get a real buzz out of it – which is quite understandable seeing as how it's the only thing they do and, by definition, are getting a sense of achievement out of the only thing they have time for. The trouble is, if you are so focused on work, you won't have the time or energy to improve your social life. In turn, you won't get a buzz out of it, leading to a vicious circle.

5 Increase your productivity, not your working hours

One of the things you discover within a short while of being at work is a weird phenomenon called 'presenteeism'. This involves people spending hour after hour at their desks – even if precious little real work actually gets done. In some workplaces, they will even leave their computers switched on and their jackets hung on the back of a chair to give the impression they haven't left yet. Yet the real trick is not to spend hours in the office but to get your work done more quickly.

Money and renting your home

One of the first things you will need to sort out when you leave college will be the question of finding somewhere new to live.

You've probably been there and done that already: most people who go to college spend at least one year outside of halls of residence. So the idea of renting a place isn't new.

But, although it may not feel like it at first, there is a big difference between sharing a place with half a dozen college friends for a few terms and finding a home that you will hopefully want to rent for a year or two at least.

While all sorts of things – damp walls, manky broken-down furniture, ancient kitchens, shabby decor, unhygienic bathrooms and so on – might have been acceptable when endured as a student, you will probably have different priorities now.

So what kind of things should you be looking for? Here are a few simple steps to help you decide on the right place for you.

Decide what you want

Before you even walk into a letting agent's office, take the time to work out what you are actually looking for. This will help you decide whether each property you view meets your requirements.

Overall, given that this is the longest period you are likely to be spending in a place since leaving your parents' home, you should spend as much time on this as if you were buying your own home.

Here are some of the things you may want to take into account.

- *How much you can afford* – This is probably the most important aspect. It is worth spending some time on a few property letting websites for your chosen area to check out what is available for your kind of budget.

- *Location* – You will have to decide between potentially conflicting factors, such as closeness to work, transport links, or where your social life is mostly based (you may want to live in an area where there is a vibrant night life, for instance). You might also want to take the general feel of the neighbourhood into account. If you face being mugged for your mobile every time you step out of the tube or off the bus, maybe this isn't the place for you.

- *What kind of accommodation* – The choice is likely to be diverse: a flat, a house, a studio, a single room. Some of the issues you may want to take into account here are your need for privacy or company, outside space, cost and comfort. Don't be afraid to consider options that might not immediately strike you as perfect: apart from anything else, you might not be able to afford exactly what you want.

- *Length of tenancy* – The longer the tenancy period, the greater the potential rent discount you might be able to negotiate. Equally, there is less flexibility if you don't like the place or your fellow-tenants, or work commitments force you to move out.

- *Furnished or unfurnished* – Again, the issues involved include cost, as well as the type of furniture available and whether you can afford to furnish the place yourself. Generally, though not always, landlords who rent unfurnished accommodation tend to be more relaxed about the overall décor, as long as you keep the place in good nick. If the place is furnished or part-furnished, check that the individual items – sofas, cookers, gas and electrical appliances – all meet new safety standards.

- *Number of bedrooms, bathrooms and living rooms* – Ideally, a three-bedroom home where individual residents are not part of the same family should have at least one additional toilet separate from the one in the main bathroom. A four-bedroom home should offer two bathrooms. In terms of living space, you should aim for somewhere to spend time in other than your own bedroom.

- *Off-street parking* – If one or more of you has a car, parking space could be useful, both in terms of security but also because many councils are increasingly charging for permits for people to park in their own streets.

- *Garden* – The benefits of having one are obvious, especially in the summer. But you may want to balance that against the cost and time involved in looking after it.

How much does it cost to rent?

Whenever you are renting, it is tempting to simply look at the weekly rent and assume that's all you will have pay if you take on a place. Big mistake.

Firstly, it is a common error to multiply a week's rent by four to arrive at how much a place will cost you every month. But in fact, you should multiply the weekly rent by 4.33 to work out how much you will pay. For example, £150 a week is £649.50 a month, not £600.

In addition to the rent itself, you should factor in:

- home contents insurance: the landlord will protect the building and all of its fixtures and fittings. But you are responsible for anything you bring into the home. In shared rental properties you are looking at between £100–£200 a year;

- council tax, or your share of it;
- utility bills, or a share of those costs. Make sure you know whether your landlord is paying for water bills: most do, but not all;
- service charges: this usually applies in cases where you live in a block of flats. If it does, find out whether you are meant to pay this, or if your landlord is;
- deposit: you will normally be expected to pay one month's rent in advance, plus one month to six weeks' rent to pay for any damages to the property. The latter is repayable to you after a full inspection of the property is carried out. You cannot offset the deposit against the last month's rent.

Where to find somewhere to live

Online – One of the easiest ways to check out properties. It is highly convenient, allows you to search among letting agents in your chosen area, plus it may offer access to photos and floor plans of individual properties.

Local newspapers and classified sections – This used to be a traditional way of finding a property. Some landlords prefer to advertise their properties privately in this way, thus avoiding having to pay fees of between 10–15 per cent to letting agents. But there is a risk that by the time you make a call on a property, it may have gone.

Letting agents – It is always worth registering with all letting agent offices in the area you want to live and asking for details of relevant houses and flats available. The chances are that their lists will be up to date. You should also be able to negotiate with them on the price of any property they have available to rent.

By the way, letting agents are no longer allowed to charge you a fee for letting a property to you. But they can charge a fee to handle administrative work, such as checking your references. These costs can range from £25 to £150.

You may also be asked to pay a 'holding deposit' of £50 to £200 or more to secure the property you want. This will subsequently be deducted from your first month's rent if you go ahead, or refunded if the landlord decides not to proceed with your tenancy. It is important to know in advance what these costs are.

Look for 'To Let' signs in your area – Driving or walking around your chosen area may sound like a bizarre idea, but it has certain advantages. It is highly likely that properties with 'To Let' signs outside are just that. You will both get to know the neighbourhood and discover if is attractive to you. Plus, you will find out which agents have the highest number of boards and therefore are most likely to have the most available properties.

Bear in mind that not all properties to let will have an advertising hoarding outside – while in some cases, unscrupulous agents have been known to put up signs outside blocks of flats, for example, where they have nothing available to rent, purely as a form of cheap advertising. When you call, they tell you that flat has gone and offer you something else.

THE RENTAL CHECKLIST

Many people find looking for a rental property so stressful that the minute they see something which vaguely meets their needs they sigh with relief and don't do the rest of their research as thoroughly as they might.

There are four key areas you should look at: the outside, inside, safety and finances.

Here is a quick checklist you may want to photocopy and take with you when looking at a property:

Outside

- What is the area like? Does it meet your needs in terms of local amenities (shops, nightlife, parks and so on) and transport links?
- Does the property look in a good state? Is it safe? Has it ever been burgled?
- What are the outside doors like? If it's a flat, is there an entry-phone or a burglar alarm?
- What are the neighbours like?
- If there is a garden, who is responsible for maintaining it?

Inside

- Is it in good condition? Check for signs of damp and flaking paint or scabby wallpaper.
- What repairs, if any, need to be carried out? Check for poor electrical wiring, faulty plugs or lights. In the bathroom and kitchen, make sure the taps are not leaking and the shower works.
- Check whether central heating is available and ask if all the radiators work. Do the same with all appliances, such as washing machines or dishwashers.
- Make sure there is enough storage for your belongings, such as clothes, books and CDs. If you ride a bike, where will you be able to store it safely?

- Are the kitchen cupboards and work surfaces suitable? What about the pots, pans and cutlery?
- Make sure there are enough electricity points. If you need broadband, ask if it is already connected or whether you have to apply for it.

Safety checks

- Do any downstairs windows have locks?
- Is there a safety blanket and fire extinguisher in the kitchen? This is not strictly required by law in every case, but may apply in some properties that have been converted into flats.
- Is there a Landlord's Gas Safety Record available to view? A landlord (or his agent) has responsibilities under the Gas Safety (Installation and Use) Regulations 1998 to arrange maintenance by a Corgi-registered installer for all pipework, appliances and flues. They must also arrange for an annual gas safety check to be carried out, keep a record of the safety check for two years and issue a copy to each existing tenant within 28 days of the check being completed and to any new tenants before they move in.
- Do the furnishings comply with the latest fire safety regulations (1989 Fire and Furniture Regulations)? Furniture that complies will always have some sort of tag saying so.
- Are there carbon monoxide detectors present? There is no legal requirement for a landlord to have these, but a cheap one can cost as little as £10 to £15. You may want to install one yourself.
- Are there enough smoke alarms? This is obligatory for properties built after 1992 and also in Scotland. Having one in the kitchen and hallway is always useful. But do note that if one is fitted, the landlord may make you responsible for ensuring that it is tested every 12 months and replacing any batteries.

Financial issues

■ How much is the rent and what does it cover?

■ What are the estimated running costs of the property? This includes gas, electricity, council tax, telephone and water bills.

■ What other bills are there and what are you liable to pay for?

■ What is the deposit required? How will it be handled?

If you decide to rent the property

It is at this point that everything has to be totally clear between you and the landlord or his or her agent.

You should ensure that any necessary repairs to the property are carried out by the landlord before you move in. Make sure this is agreed in writing.

Don't be shy about double-checking the inventory list: at the end of the day, your deposit may be affected if you agreed to items being there when they weren't.

Having agreed the amount and issues with the landlord, you will be asked for some information about yourself. Be prepared for it to be very thorough: the landlord is trying to protect the property from people who may be less than keen to look after it to the same standards as he or she does. Many landlords will also have had painful experiences of tenants who are unwilling to pay their rent on time, or at all.

Note that if you fail any of the checks, you may not always get your administration fee back, so check this out with the letting agent before agreeing to hand over any cash or signing any forms.

Here are some of the things you may be asked for:

references from previous landlords – you may be asked to give the details of where you have
     lived within the last three years;
a credit check – this will allow them to see if you have a good history of paying your bills;
your bank details – including bank name, account number and sort code;
details of your employment – your employer, job title, payroll number, salary, previous
     employer over the past three years and so on.

As a younger tenant, you may be asked to provide a guarantor's name. A guarantor – your parents, for example – will be contractually liable, both financially and legally, should you fail to pay the rent during your tenancy or in the event of damage to the property.

Normally it takes about 10 working days to take up and confirm references, clear your cheque covering the first rent period and the deposit, arrange for inventories and the transfer of utility accounts into your name. No agent should allow you possession before all this has been done.

The tenancy agreement

You will be asked to sign a legally binding agreement between yourself and the landlord, applicable only to you and the property you are renting, that states the amount of rent, the length of the tenancy, your rights and responsibilities.

Your agreement will most probably be an *assured* or *assured shorthold* tenancy under the Housing Act 1988. Most agents require an agreement to be for a minimum of six months and rarely write a tenancy agreement for longer than a year.

If you want to stay on, or leave early

Tenancies are frequently renewed and agents often agree the terms for renewal at the beginning and include them in the tenancy agreement. If you're likely to leave before the end of the original term agreed, you must negotiate possible break clauses to be written into the agreement.

For example, you can agree an annual lease with a six-month break clause, which can be triggered by either side one month before the six months are up. This gives you leeway to move on or the landlord leeway to move you out if things aren't working between you.

If there is no break clause, you remain responsible for the rent until the end of the term agreed, unless a new and satisfactory tenant can be found. Sometimes landlords may agree to let you off if they find a new tenant, but they don't have to.

How to keep your deposit safe

For many tenants, the issue of how their deposit will be looked after is of critical importance. After all, the chances are that they will be asked to hand over hundreds of pounds, perhaps even £1,500 or more, as a deposit to a landlord, supposedly to make sure the property does not suffer damage and any possessions in it are unharmed.

But in the past, many tenants have complained that they rarely got back all – sometimes any – of the deposit they handed over to their landlord. In recent years, however, the situation has changed.

Since April 2007, all deposits (up to £25,000 annual rent) taken by landlords and letting agents for assured shorthold tenancies in England and Wales must be protected by a tenancy deposit protection scheme.

What are tenancy deposit schemes?

These schemes allow tenants to get all or part of their deposit back when they are entitled to it and encourage tenants and landlords to make a clear agreement from the start on the condition of the property.

There are two types of tenancy deposit protection schemes:

1   *Insurance-based schemes:* the landlord keeps the deposit and pays the insurance scheme to insure against the landlord failing to repay the tenant any money due to him or her.

2   *Custodial schemes:* Money is held by the scheme until it is time for it to be repaid at the end of the tenancy. The custodial scheme is free to use. The landlord simply puts the deposit into the scheme at the beginning of the tenancy.

From the tenant's point of view, the precise type of scheme matters less than the fact that your money is protected.

Within 14 days of taking the deposit, the landlord must have provided you with details of how the deposit is being protected, including:

- the landlord's contact details
- contact details of the tenancy deposit scheme
- information explaining the purpose of the deposit
- how to apply for the release of the deposit
- what to do if there is a dispute about the deposit

Clearly, tenants have a responsibility to return the property in the same condition as they took it on. This means that when you move out, both the contents in the property and its condition should be checked against the agreement made when you moved in. The landlord or agent then agrees with the tenant how much of the deposit will be returned to them and this money must be returned within 10 days.

If there is a dispute as to how much of the deposit is being withheld, each of the schemes operates an Alternative Dispute Resolution (ADR) system, to which you can complain. The ADR system, which is free to tenants, decides on a fair amount of deposit – if any – that may be retained by the landlord.

Clearly, if you are unhappy with this solution, you can still go to court to get legal satisfaction there.

Your landlord or the letting agent will tell you about the kind of deposit scheme they are using. If they don't, make sure you ask for details.

Making a complaint

Very occasionally, things can go wrong. If you have a complaint about the conduct of an agent, you can contact the Ombudsman for Estate Agents (OEA). Go to www.oea.co.uk.

The OEA provides an independent service for dealing with a dispute between member estate agents and consumers who are actual or potential buyers or sellers of residential property in the UK.

The OEA will advise on alternative routes to take if the estate agent you wish to complain about is not a member. You can also contact the local council's trading standards department.

Renting with others – the ground rules

The chances are that you will have had some experience of living with others while at college. The difference between then and now is that the stakes are higher: this isn't just for a few months and while you definitely want to get on well with your flat or housemates, you also have to go to work during the week. So finding someone compatible and agreeing some ground rules makes sense.

What kind of things might you want to consider?

How the bills will be paid: This could include details of, for example, how you will divide up and pay the rent and household bills. These might include gas, electricity, telephone, insurance, TV licence and also food, cleaning products, toiletries and other day-to-day expenses.

Whose name will the bills be in? How will you divide the payments? You may wish to open a joint account to set aside the money for the rent and other bills, with everyone paying the same amount into the account.

Being a good flat or housemate: once you've sorted out all the official stuff, you may want to lay down a few more rules here. Living with others involves a lot of compromise, so guidelines can help prevent arguments later on.

For example, you may want to decide who will be responsible for the washing, cooking, cleaning and other domestic chores, or whether to ask your other flat and housemates before inviting friends to stay.

Remember that no matter how hard you try, there will be things about your flat or housemates that you end up not liking – and vice versa.

It could be things like buying toilet paper, doing the washing up, bills and money, cleaning or even sexual habits. It is amazing how many people get petty over seemingly insignificant things once they have been living together for a while.

Contacts and links

Directgov: for an overview of your rights, plus many helpful links to other websites where you can get more advice, visit www.direct.gov.uk/en/HomeAndCommunity/index.htm

National Association of Estate Agents: www.naea.co.uk

Council of Mortgage Lenders: www.cml.org.uk

HousePriceCrash: www.housepricecrash.co.uk

Money and your car

It is an almost inevitable fact that at some stage in their lives, almost everyone asks themselves whether they should buy a car. There are both advantages and disadvantages to owning a car.

Pluses
On the plus side there is the massive convenience of having one, the opportunity to travel anywhere you want, at any time, without having to wonder about timetables or lost connections. Your travel is door-to-door, which means a lot less hassle and can often be much quicker.

If you travel in the same vehicle with a group of people, using a car can be surprisingly cheap, at least in terms of petrol costs.

Minuses
The biggest downside of car ownership is that it is a money pit. We're not just talking about the cost of buying the vehicle, which can run into thousands of pounds. There's also maintenance and repairs, insurance and road tax.

Don't forget to budget for unforeseen charges, such as parking (or fines if you don't pay for a ticket), not to mention paying for speeding and other motoring offences.

Finally, don't forget about depreciation, which means your car will be worth anything up to one third less every year, regardless of whether you bought it new or secondhand.

The AA's own figures suggest that the annual cost of owning a car which was bought for under £10,000 is about £2,000 a year – and that's before you even turn over the ignition key. Actually running it will cost another 40p a mile, assuming you drive about 10,000 miles a year.

Then there are the environmental issues to consider, not least the damage caused by building cars, as well as running them: a 100-mile journey in a small car causes 20.5 kg of CO_2 emissions, as compared to 4.7 kg travelling the same distance on a bus.

Are you sure you still want to own a car?

Thought so. OK, here's what you need to do if you are going to buy one.

Three simple steps before you buy a car

As with almost any other purchase, it pays to sit down first and work out what kind of car you are likely to need.

Decide what you can afford or want to pay. This is probably the most important aspect of buying a car. After all, there is little point in lusting after something if you can't afford it. So set yourself a limit in terms of what you can pay and stick to that.

Generally speaking, you should aim to keep within about 8–12 per cent of your gross annual earnings, taking a repayment period of about three years into account. So for a £25,000 annual salary, you can buy a car worth up to

£3,000. That doesn't sound like much, but bear in mind that you will have to pay hefty running costs, of which more later. OK, so it may not be the car you really want, but you won't break the bank buying or running it and, with a bit of luck, in three years' time you should be able to do much better.

Decide what you want. This can involve a wide variety of 'sub-choices'. For example:

- Is it largely for short or long journeys?
- Do you want a smaller engine for economy or a larger one for power (the former is cheaper)?
- How many doors do you want (three is cheaper than five, but five is more convenient)?
- Do you prefer diesel to petrol (most experts suggest that to get the full benefits of diesel, which costs more to buy, you need to travel more than 12,000 miles a year)?
- Automatic or manual gears (surveys suggests autos cause less stress when driving, but manuals give greater control and also cost slightly less to maintain)?
- Will you be carrying other adults or lots of stuff (you will have to find a car with more legroom, or an estate, or a car with a large enough roof rack)?

Think about depreciation and running costs. Depreciation in the first year can range from more than 40 per cent on some popular models to around 12 per cent on others. Over three years, according to *Which?* magazine, the value can drop between 50 and 77 per cent.

As for running costs, a survey by the AA found the following costs for cars within five different price brackets:

Petrol car running costs – basic guide based on 2008 prices

Running costs

	Cost new (£s)				
	up to 10,000	10,000 to 13,000	13,000 to 20,000	20,000 to 30,000	over 30,000
Standing charges per annum (£s)					
Road tax	120.0	145.0	170.0	210.0	400.0
Insurance	420.0	472.0	606.0	810.0	961.0
Cost of capital	401.0	578.0	806.0	1245.0	1835.0
Depreciation (at 10,000 miles/annum)	1097.0	1636.0	2486.0	3247.0	7099.0
Breakdown cover	45.0	45.0	45.0	45.0	45.0
Total (£s)	2083.00	2876.00	4113.00	5557.00	10340.00
Standing charges per mile (pence)					
5,000	41.22	56.86	81.26	109.84	203.96
10,000	20.83	28.76	41.13	55.57	103.40
15,000	14.18	19.61	28.08	37.91	70.83
20,000	10.96	15.20	21.81	29.41	55.25
25,000	8.86	12.29	17.64	23.79	44.77
30,000	7.42	10.30	14.79	19.93	37.54
Running costs per mile (pence)					
Petrol*	10.84	11.58	13.62	16.18	19.46
Tyres	0.52	0.68	1.03	1.68	1.96
Service labour costs	3.2	2.94	2.79	2.91	3.22
Replacement parts	1.67	1.75	1.88	3.03	3.35
Parking and tolls	1.8	1.8	1.8	1.8	1.8

Source: AA

*Unleaded petrol at 90.9 pence/litre

TOP TIP

Bear in mind that depreciation is also affected by factors such as the very colour and finish of a car. Believe it or not, that £500 spent on a metallic finish may well be worth £2,000 more than a model with a flat finish one year down the line, according to EurotaxGlass's, the well-known car price guide.

AA research shows that six out of 10 new cars are blue, red or silver. Buyers tend to gravitate to those colours because most are innately 'conservative'. This means if you want to buy a car more cheaply, go for one in an unusual colour, like yellow or mauve. If you want to sell one more easily in three years, stick to a boring shade.

Buying the car

Let's assume you have chosen the car you want and that – unless the tooth fairy has paid you a visit – you are buying a used model. Where do you go to buy it? There are several places you can choose.

Franchised dealers. These have the closest relationship with manufacturers. Their prices are likely to be high but also very negotiable, in that among the payments they receive from manufacturers are rewards purely for shifting cars through the salesroom. They should offer a good warranty, excellent after-sales service and many of their cars will have a thorough pre-sales inspection and all faults should have been fixed.

Independent dealers. They will sell used cars from more than one manufacturer, which will tend to be older. Prices may be lower and you should get a better trade-in deal if you already have a car, as they are more likely to sell it themselves than trade it off. But some cars may not have as thorough a service.

Car supermarkets. Increasingly common, or at least they claim to be. The term applies to dealers with many hundreds of cars available, sometimes up to 1,000 at a time. The choice is very great and prices are cheap, but that leaves little to haggle over. Test drives are less common and servicing prior to sales is less thorough. You have to know what you are buying.

Auctions. These can either take place at giant one-day sales, where hundreds of cars will pass under the hammer in a matter of minutes, or online through websites like eBay. The advantage is that prices can be ultra-cheap: many dealers go there for their own cars, albeit at more restricted trade auctions.

But you are more likely to be 'buying blind' and you really need both to do your prior research incredibly carefully on price and to take someone with you who knows a lot about cars. Your legal rights are also less than if you buy from a dealer. Finally, DO NOT buy a car online without seeing it, not unless you want to risk thousands of pounds.

Private sale. Buying off a private individual allows you to pick and choose between any models advertised the UK. You will also get the lowest prices of all. But you won't get any warranty or after-sales service and your legal rights are restricted if something goes wrong with the car after you buy it.

Negotiating the right price

Buying a car at the right price is one of the most daunting tasks any individual will face. Not only do you have to make sure that you are not buying a mechanical lemon, but also that you are not paying over the odds for it. There are several easy steps to help ensure you do not make a terrible mistake.

Check either the Glass's or Parker's online price guides. For about £3–£4 both will allow you to input the precise make and model of your car (sometimes even the car's own registration number), along with its mileage, and tell you what it might fetch. The price will distinguish between what you might expect to pay to a dealer (more) or to a private individual (less). Go to www.glass.co.uk or www.parkers.co.uk.

Bear in mind that the prices given are not 100 per cent accurate. In recent months, values of second-hand vehicles have been falling rapidly, mostly as a result of the credit crunch. This means you should be able to shave a few hundred pounds off the guide price.

See the car with someone who knows about them. There is no substitute for experience, so take someone with you. If you don't know anyone, the AA provides a service starting from about £165, which offers a full vehicle inspection.

If you do take the DIY inspection route, make sure you do a very thorough check of the tyres, brakes, seatbelts, locks, the paintwork, the oil level and so on, and remember to listen out for strange noises.

Finally, check out the MOT certificate and all servicing bills and the main service document. You want to ensure all servicing was carried out regularly, as per the manufacturer's instructions.

Negotiate the price. Assuming you are satisfied by all the other points, this is the hard part – or at least, what many people assume to be the hard part. In fact, if the car is fine mechanically, the bodywork is good and you have researched the market for that particular model carefully, there is no reason why you should not do well.

Bear in mind that the seller will probably have done some homework and should be roughly in the same ballpark area that you are. In which case, when discussing price, mention any small problems - scuffed wheel rims, dirty seats, lights not fully working - and add that the guide books are not currently reflecting the state of today's motoring market.

Aim for 10-20 per cent lower than the Glass's/Parker's guide price for a vehicle in the right condition and be prepared to settle for about 10 per cent or so. You might be able to screw the seller down further, but ask yourself whether it's worth sweating over a couple of hundred quid.

Paying for the car

According to survey carried out several years ago by the Financial Services Authority, the financial watchdog, people spend many hours researching what car to buy before even venturing into a show room. When they are there, most will make a final decision within 30 minutes.

Yet when it comes to deciding how to pay for a car, most end up choosing the dealer's own finance package, even though it may well cost them at least £1,000 more over the period they end up owning it.

If you want the best purchase deal for your car, here are the options - and what factors you should consider when deciding between them.

Hire purchase

This is a deal typically available from car dealers. It combines elements of both a loan and a lease. In essence, you make an initial deposit on the car then pay off the balance in monthly instalments over an agreed period of time. At the end of this period, the car is yours.

The contract is actually between you and the lender, usually a bank or broker, but is normally arranged by the dealer. The lender effectively buys the vehicle and allows you to use it while you make payments. Only when all payments are complete is the car officially yours.

Pros

■ You can buy something you couldn't otherwise afford.

■ You are more likely to obtain this finance as the lender has some 'security' in the form of your car – this is sometimes reflected in better interest rates.

■ The car can be yours, or rather, driven by you out of the showroom within minutes of telling the salesperson you want it.

Cons

■ The car is not yours until the final instalment is paid and can be repossessed for any missed payment before then.

■ Reselling the car during the hire purchase term can be complicated. You will still need to pay off the money you owe in full, as you will if the car is written off in an accident.

■ You may be liable for early settlement fees and 'option to purchase' fees. These are not mandatory on hire purchase agreements, but will be charged by some dealers.

■ Interest rates can be high.

Bank or building society loans

Here, you obtain a loan directly from the financial institution before proceeding with the purchase. You agree with the lender how much you can borrow and the repayment period. The interest charged, agreed at the outset, depends on the sum involved: until recently, the more you borrowed, the lower the interest rate paid.

Pros

- The purchase will incur less interest, because you are able to shop around widely and get the best loan deal in the market.
- You can set the amount of time you need to repay the loan.
- The car cannot be repossessed simply because you miss one or two payments.

Cons

- Loans are harder to come by right now and interest rates are rising, especially since sales of payment protection policies linked to the loans – and which contribute a large slice of lender' profits – are to be tightly regulated.
- You may have to pay a redemption penalty if you pay the loan off early.
- If more than one application for a loan is refused, you may end up damaging your credit history.

Credit cards

Believe it or not, it is sometimes possible to borrow enough money to buy a car with a credit card. All you need is a 0 per cent credit card on purchases and a large enough line of credit.

Pros

- With a 0 per cent card for, say, 12 months, you are effectively being loaned several thousands of pounds at no interest. Even in December 2008, at the height of the credit crunch, there were more than 30 cards offering 0 per cent on purchases for period between three and 12 months.
- You can use the card to buy the car, make as many payments as possible during the interest-free period, then take out a loan to repay the rest of what you owe. This cuts down your total interest payments.

Cons

- You need to be very disciplined to do this. For many people, the temptation to keep spending up to the limit of the card is too great. When the interest-free period runs out, they end up paying a much higher rate of interest on their debts.

Personal contract purchase (PCP)

PCP deals are often offered by large car franchises and manufacturers themselves. You pay a deposit and then make monthly payments for up to 36 months while continuing to use the car. At the end of the loan period, you return it to the owner or you buy it outright by paying a final lump sum.

Pros

- Because the car still has a residual value at the end of the lease period, it means that you usually make lower monthly payments.
- PCPs reduce the headache of car maintenance problems, insofar as the car you have a contract out on is new and will still be under warranty for most of the contract period.

Cons

- The initial deposit is often quite large.
- Mileage is usually restricted – to 10,000 miles a year for example. Go over that limit and you must pay a large final payment, even if you don't end up owning the car.
- You will never actually own the car unless you make a very large 'balloon payment' of up to one third of the purchase price. In practice, people end up being rolled into new PCP contracts ad infinitum.

Contacts and links

What Car: also has masses of car reviews, plus a quick – and free – service that tells you how much a second-hand car might be worth. Find it at www.whatcar.com

Honest John: this is the website of a former car dealer and regular *Daily Telegraph* columnist, with masses of useful information about cars, including reviews, prices and even places to go to for cheap deals. Go to www.honestjohn.co.uk

5 Money and holidays

Every year, up to 20 million of us jet off to supposedly sunnier climes. Depending on which survey you believe, we are likely to spend between £650 and £800 per person for our fortnight in the sun.

The likelihood is that at least £100 of that amount will be wasted, not so much in terms of the silly knick-knacks we come home with, but the poor deals we end up with when planning our holiday.

Here are a few rules to follow before going abroad.

Get the right insurance

A lot of disputes happen because people think they are covered and discover too late that they are not. In particular, look out for:

- maximum individual limits on each item you can claim for;
- excesses: if the excess is £50 per item, that's £50 for the camera, £50 for the money, £50 for the passport and so on;
- the extent of medical protection you have: this matters if you are likely to be on holiday in countries, like the US, where the cost of care can be very high. Some experts argue that you need at least £2m of cover, plus two or three times that amount in liability insurance, in case you get sued;
- any exclusions on the policy, such as pre-existing medical conditions;
- whether cash is included and how much;
- whether loss is covered along with theft;

■ whether 24-hour emergency assistance is available.

Avoid 'foreign usage fees' – use the right credit card

Nationwide Building Society suggests that travellers face being charged more than £500m in foreign usage fees by their credit or debit card provider.

This is because almost all cardholders face a minimum charge of 2.75 per cent in so-called 'foreign usage fees', plus a further 2 per cent if they choose to withdraw their money from overseas cash machines. The only cards that do not apply this charge on purchases in Europe are the Post Office, Saga and Liverpool Victoria's card, which has now been taken over by Barclaycard.

Watch out for so-called 'dynamic currency conversion'

This is most often used in restaurants and some shops in Europe. This immediately converts the price you pay for an item into sterling at the terminal itself – and leads to a very poor exchange rate. You can, however, insist on paying in the local currency with your card.

Your bill is then converted into sterling by your bank at a later date – and at an exchange rate more favourable to you. You also don't pay anything up to £3 for the conversion to take place at the terminal.

Change your money well before leaving

If you ignore this advice, you may well end up paying up to 10 per cent more for your foreign currency at the airport. There are three main places where you can buy it before you go.

1   Online, with Travelex. This is one of the largest bureaux de change in the UK. Its website promises to be the most competitive and can be found here: www.travelex.co.uk. Do not confuse prices on the website with what you will have to pay at one of Travelex's airport booths, however, which are far more expensive.

2   Regular surveys show that Marks & Spencer offers one of the best deals on foreign currency and most of the company's stores have a department where it is possible to order it – and often walk away with it on the same day. You can also order online (www.marksandspencer.com) or call 0870 600 3502.

3   Failing that, you can also get a reasonable deal at the Post Office. You can either order over the counter or go to its website and order your money online.

If you are going off the beaten track, consider traveller's cheques

If lost or stolen, traveller's cheques can be replaced with a single telephone call – usually within 24 hours. Additionally, American Express now also provides help with getting a stolen or lost passport re-issued.

However, it can often be difficult to cash traveller's cheques in remote places. Even so, dollar cheques are sometimes useful in the US, where they are widely accepted as payment for goods and services.

Note that some banks in the US levy heavy charges to convert traveller's cheques into hard currency. Similarly, some European banks will charge up to 6 per cent commission.

Also, while some overseas currency exchange outlets don't charge, they may offer a lower rate of exchange.

Check your mobile phone charges

Mobile telephones are among the top five most popular travelling items taken overseas and are a good way of staying in touch with your family and friends back home.

The network service that allows you to use your UK mobile phone abroad is called 'international roaming'.

Contact your UK mobile network provider to ensure your phone allows you to make calls from abroad and how much it costs – some providers are very expensive.

In 2007, the European Union agreed a cap on roaming charges, forcing many operators to bring their prices down. From 2009, if you use your overseas phone to make a call, you should pay no more than 0.43 Euros (about 40p as at March 2009) per minute, or 0.19 Euros (17p) to receive a call.

Some mobile services offer cheaper calls abroad in return for a monthly fee – check with your network provider what the costs are and how long you would be committed to paying for the service.

Another way round the problem is to use a SIM card from a foreign network in your own phone. They can be bought abroad at international airports and holiday destinations or, for some European countries, from some UK retailers. You can find them quite easily online.

Alternatively, consider renting a mobile phone from a telephone company in the country you are visiting.

Money and love

If there is one thing virtually guaranteed to happen to you at this point in your life, it is that you will fall in love.

Maybe you already have: you met the love of your life at college and are still together, making a go of it now that you are both out in the real world. If not, it is sure to happen at some stage in the coming years.

But amid all the ecstasy and the euphoria, it makes sense to stand back a little and work a few things out with your partner. It is possible that you may be unlike each other when it comes to managing money. A few ground rules agreed at the start can avoid painful disagreements months or years down the line.

Should the worst happen and your relationship breaks up, it is important to make sure that even if you do both come out of it with your hearts broken, at least you won't suffer too much financially.

So how is it possible to do this?

There are a few steps you should always follow.

■ Be completely honest with your partner at the outset. If you are going to live together, discuss how you each feel about spending money, obtaining credit, paying bills on time, being in debt and all the other financial activities that are likely to come up in your daily lives. It may be that you are a better money manager, or maybe your partner is. Either way, agree some ground rules you can both observe and stick to them.

49

- Make sure that you agree in advance exactly how all the bills are going to be shared out between you. A joint account, into which you both pay an amount from your own personal accounts and from which household bills are paid, is a starting point. It may not always be the same amount, especially if one of you earns a lot more than the other. Or you may prefer to keep your financial independence and retain control of your earnings over and above any joint bills.

- Do not agree to be the guarantor for any of each other's loans or credit agreements, as you may end up being made responsible for them if the other person is unable to pay. In the early stages, if either of you wants to buy an expensive item, for example a car, make sure the ground rules cover what happens to it if anything should happen, including sickness, unemployment or a relationship breakdown. One simple thing worth agreeing is that neither of you will apply for credit without discussing it first with the other.

- If you decide to buy a house, an agreement over who pays what and in whose name the property is placed becomes essential. This includes how much each of you will put in as a deposit, plus legal and other purchase costs; also, as with rentals, how you'll pay the bills, including the mortgage, insurance and utilities.

- Always keep your own independence. This means a separate credit card and savings account, particularly if you are not married. It also means making sure that you know exactly how much money is being spent jointly and where your money is going.

- If you are at the stage where you know you will be spending a large part of your life together, protection becomes an issue, especially in the event of a joint home purchase. You should definitely be thinking about life insurance to help pay off the mortgage in the event of one of you dying and possibly other cover against sickness, particularly if you are going to have children together.

- Think about making a will: this is especially important if you are not married, as the UK's intestacy laws mean there is no provision for a surviving life partner. If there are no children then the estate passes to the parents, siblings and other relatives in a specified order.

Gay couples who live together also have no special legal rights against each other unless they have registered their relationship as a civil partnership under the Civil Partnerships Act.

Relationship breakdown

Ideally it would be nice if, in the event of relationship breakdown, all financial issues were to be settled amicably by both parties, regardless of any emotional pain involved.

In practice, precisely because of that emotional pain, it is possible that you may find it harder than expected to resolve those issues.

What you should definitely do is as follows.

- If you have a joint account, write to your bank immediately, informing them of your new single status. Consider closing the account or taking your name off if you do not have an agreement on how joint bills will be paid in future.
- Cancel any joint credit cards – for obvious reasons.
- Ensure that your salary payments go directly into your personal account. You can always transfer money to pay for bills, but if your income is paid into a joint account, your ex could access it and clean you out.

- Discuss and agree the issue of joint savings with your ex-partner: as they will be in both your names, the chances are they cannot be withdrawn without both your consent. This increases your chances of a fair split.

- If your partner has bought and is paying for joint assets in his or her name, for example a car, while you paid other bills, try to agree who gets to keep them going forward, presumably in return for taking on any future bills.

- If a property is involved, dig out any contract you have agreed between you and talk to a lawyer right away.

- It is possible that, even though you are both likely to be in your 20s, one or both of you has been saving into a pension. In theory, there are pension-sharing laws in the event of splitting up and recent court cases have left the issue of whether they apply to non-married couples in a bit of a grey area. But given that it is unlikely either of you will have built up a sizeable pension pot at this stage, it may make more sense just to call this one quits.

PART II

Credit and Debt

7 Money and credit

Each year, more than 300,000 graduates leave higher education, armed with a degree or a similar qualification.

Many will also leave college owing thousands, sometimes tens of thousands, of pounds to their banks, credit card providers and the Student Loans Company (SLC), not to mention their parents – all of whom helped finance their studies.

Although a minority manage to get through their three or four years at college and survive without falling into too much debt, for most the reality is different. The chances are you are in the latter category.

For almost all graduates, therefore, the issue of debt, as well as that of obtaining credit when they first start work, will play a major role for at least their first decade after leaving university. It can condition their choice of jobs, their future spending patterns and, therefore, their lifestyle options.

Although this is rarely acknowledged, growing levels of indebtedness faced by graduates compared with their counterparts 20 or 30 years ago also helps influence other decisions, such as when to get married, buy a first home and even when to have children.

This section aims to help you make key decisions about credit and debt: when to take it on, how much to borrow, what kind of credit is best – and which types to avoid – as well as how to pay it back more quickly.

Finally, if you are beginning to find serious problems with the levels of debt you are in, there will hopefully be some answers for you in terms of what you can do and where to turn to for help.

Student loans

The starting point for any graduate must be their student loan. For most, this is the largest amount they will be able to borrow from any single source, especially if they live away from home.

The money comes from the Student Loans Company (SLC), a government-backed organisation which lends money to students and then arranges for them to pay it back when they are in work later on. Different arrangements are in place for Scotland, where the Student Awards Agency for Scotland channels funding for students studying both there and in other parts of the UK.

Regardless of where you have been studying or the source of your student loan, the amount of money you end up owing can be massive. Someone who completes a three-year course in London, where living costs are higher, and borrowed the maximum amount currently available could end up almost £19,000 in debt. Even studying outside London could leave someone owing more than £15,000.

So the key issue is how to pay that money back.

Paying back money to the Student Loans Company

Whether you like it or not, the SLC operates a system for clawing back the money you owe, which has evolved over time.

The current system works like a form of 'graduate tax'. Basically, anyone in the UK tax system has their repayments deducted at source by their employer or through their self-assessed tax returns. This is done by allocating all SLC borrowers a special National Insurance number when they first apply for the loan. The SLC instructs HM Revenue & Customs (HMRC) to tell the borrower, or their employer, when repayments are due to start. From that point on, all due repayments are deducted from taxable earnings, collected by HMRC and allocated to the borrower's loan balance.

Just before the amount owed is expected to be fully repaid, HMRC notifies the borrower, or their employer, that repayments should stop. Any unnecessary repayments made after the loan is paid up will be refunded.

Currently repayments are 9 per cent of all before-tax earnings above £15,000. If you earn £16,000 your repayments are £90 a year, but if you are on £25,000 a year, your payments rise to £810 a year, or £67.50 a month.

TOP TIP

Although the authorities say they keep a close eye on repayments and will stop you overpaying, there have been cases where people have not been notified that their payments were complete. As a result, money continued to be deducted from their salaries long after their student loans were repaid.

Although you will be refunded, no interest is payable on any overpayments. So it is worthwhile keeping an eye on how you are doing, by phoning up the SLC from time to time and checking where your account stands.

Interest on your student loan debt

Don't make the mistake of thinking that every penny of your repayments reduces the capital you owe: interest is added to the debt.

Thankfully, the rate of interest charged on student loans is not extortionate. It is based on the rate of inflation for the previous year, as calculated in March. You pay the new rate in September.

WHEN ARE LOANS WIPED CLEAN?

Loans taken between 1998 and September 2006:

- when you reach 65
- if you become permanently unfit to work
- when you die

Loans taken after September 2006:

- if they're not repaid 25 years from the first April of graduation
- if you become permanently unfit to work
- when you die

Should you pay off your student loan early?

The general advice is that while you will have to pay off your student loan at some point (unless you earn less than £15,000, of course), there is little point in paying it off early.

The reason is that student loan debts are one of the cheapest forms of long-term credit currently available (with the exception of 0 per cent interest cards, which are for limited periods only). Technically, you are not paying any 'real' interest on that debt, because the interest rate is set at the rate of inflation.

In fact, given that with luck your salary ought to be rising faster than inflation, certainly in the early stages of your career, your earnings will be going up faster than the rate at which interest is charged on your debt.

By the way, credit reference agencies don't hold data on student loans, so if you do apply for any other type of credit and your rating is checked, the fact you have an outstanding student loan debt shouldn't make any difference to your credit score.

TOP TIP

Assuming you have paid off more expensive debts such as credit cards, if you have money to spare it may make more sense for you to set up a tax-free ISA savings account rather than paying back a student loan quickly.

That's because these accounts may pay more interest to savers than it costs you to service the student loan debt. So you could, in theory, save money in the ISA and use that money to pay off the debt.

Be careful with your strategy, though. If you are saving for a deposit on a house, say, it may make more sense to have a larger lump sum to put down in a few years' time than paying off a low-interest debt a little earlier.

Exceptions to this

Although this strategy makes sense in most cases, there are exceptions.

- You may be someone who hates taking on debt of any sort and would rather pay back what you owe as quickly as possible. There's nothing wrong with that.
- If you are applying for a loan based on how much you can afford to repay – and increasing numbers of loans are, especially mortgages – you will be asked to provide details of current commitments. As your student loan repayments reduce your effective disposable income, this may in turn affect the maximum cash you may be able to borrow.

Moving abroad

Many former students travel abroad for a while after college; others take a sabbatical after a few years at work.

If this sounds like you and you intend to be abroad for more than three months, tell the Student Loans Company so it can calculate whether you need to make any payments while you are away and, if so, how much. The SLC has worked out roughly what you may need to pay back while living in a variety of countries, taking into account both your salary while out there and the local cost of living.

There are penalties for moving overseas and not telling the SLC. These can include demanding repayments based on an income equal to twice UK average earnings, or ordering you to repay the total loan in a single lump sum. It makes more sense to tell them where you intend to be, for how long and whether you will be earning anything while there.

Bank debts from student days

Given how much effort banks put into advertising their generous interest-free overdrafts while you are at college, no one should be surprised that bank debt forms such a large proportion of the overall amount you probably owe upon graduation.

One reason they do this is because they know that, while you may be hard up as a student and for a while after, almost all graduates eventually settle down and become responsible citizens. Sooner or later, they do pay off their debts – and so will you.

Most significantly, the banks also know that by treating students relatively well now, they get to keep them as customers for decades to come. Statistics show that each year barely 4 per cent of people switch current accounts, regardless of how dissatisfied they may be with their current bank. Bear that fact in mind, because it may come in useful later.

If you are one of those seduced by the large overdraft offered by your bank while you were at university – not to mention the free CDs, book discounts and student railcard – what happens next?

Graduate accounts

All the banks will at some point switch your student account into an ordinary current account, thus removing your interest-free overdraft. This could significantly reduce your overdraft facility, resulting in high penalty charges being applied to your account.

That said, most will tend to convert your account gradually, reducing the amount of interest-free loan over a period of several years.

Typically in the first year after graduation, the maximum interest-free overdraft is £2,000. This falls to £1,000 in the second year after graduation and £500 in the third year, reducing to zero thereafter.

Other banks operate slightly different schemes, for example offering a larger interest-free overdraft for one year after graduation but reverting immediately afterwards to a standard rate. This option might appeal to those who prefer a dose of 'cold turkey' with regard to their debts, making a significant sacrifice to pay them off over the first 12 months after leaving college.

Another option on offer at the time of writing (from one major high street bank) is a graduate account, which offers an overdraft facility of £3,000 at 0 per cent (reducing over five years from graduation) – albeit with a fee of £5 a month, or £60 a year. However, if you had to pay an *authorised* overdraft rate on the extra £1,000, as you would with the other banks, it would cost up to £178 in interest, more than off setting the £60 fee – plus you get free mobile phone cover and roadside assistance.

However, this can work both ways, as always. If you go over the limit on this account, you would face that bank's punitive unauthorised overdraft charges. Most other accounts allow you to borrow further amounts in excess of your 0 per cent allowance at their significantly lower *authorised* overdraft rates – as long as you organise it in advance

The important point is that no single account is best for every graduate. It is up to you to shop around for what suits you best after leaving college. To find out more, simply go online and do a bit of research: there are loads of websites with details of what each post-student account offers. Here are some points to consider.

- If you feel able to manage your account successfully over a period of a few years, go for a 'standard' graduate account which gradually reduces the interest-free amount you had as a student over a period of three years.
- If you want to go 'cold turkey' and pay it all back in one year – or if you owe a larger interest-free debt than the £2,000 usually available in year one – choose an account that offers that option.
- If your debt is so large that you will need both a significant interest-free overdraft and several years in which to pay it off, an account offering such an option while levying a fee may be better for you.

Probably most significantly, many former students' spending is likely to be erratic after leaving college, often for perfectly understandable reasons.

If this sounds like you, make sure you check out both a bank's authorised and unauthorised overdraft rates before plumping for any account it offers. It is a fact that a key 'profit centre' for banks consists of former students: they end up paying a significant proportion of all overdraft charges for years after graduating.

You don't have to be among them.

Graduate and career development loans

Many students graduate from university and hit the jobs market, only to discover that the qualification they obtained is of limited use in their chosen line of work. Alternatively, they may want to change career while still young enough, perhaps because they made a mistake when going to college in the first place, or they have been made redundant – hardly unusual in today's uncertain economic climate.

In such cases, the search is on for the additional funding needed to retrain, or to gain that extra qualification. One traditional way of getting over that hurdle has been by obtaining a career development loan, or CDL.

How career development loans work

CDLs are effectively underwritten by the Department for Education and Skills (DES). They allow you to borrow between £300 and £8,000 from one of three banks taking part in the scheme: Royal Bank of Scotland, Barclays and the Co-operative Bank.

The money must be used to attend a vocational course of further study, for which you can borrow up to 80 per cent of course fees, expenses including childcare, and living costs for full-time students. If you have been unemployed for at least three months, you can apply for 100 per cent of your course fees.

Applicants must be over 18 and planning to work within the EU. The course itself can be a full-time, part-time or distance course, lasting up to two years. It can also cover an additional year of work experience, if this is part of the course, though if you are eligible for a normal student loan or an employer training award you can't get a CDL.

If you want a career loan, you go to one of these three banks and agree the amount you need and how long for. Barclays and Royal Bank of

Scotland start accepting applications three months before your course start date. The Co-op starts six weeks before.

You may have to wait two to three weeks for an answer from the bank. You can't apply to more than one bank at a time.

In exceptional circumstances you can apply after you have started your course, but there needs to be enough time to process your application before the course ends.

While you are a student and for one month after your course finishes, the DES pays the interest on your loan, after which you start paying back the loan yourself.

Are they worth applying for?

Every year, many thousands of people apply for and receive career development loans. Sadly, however, they are often not worth it in their current form.

The rates charged on these loans are sometimes very expensive and in some cases misleading. For example, some brochures claim to charge a rate of interest of just 10 per cent APR. But as some experts point out, the rate is calculated by adding in not just the repayment period but the time spent on the course itself. Over the period when you actually pay back the loan, the APR can be much higher.

There is a way round the issue: many personal loan providers charge a much lower rate of interest on their deals to borrowers. But a personal loan will not give you the 'repayment holiday' that a CDL does: you would have to begin repayments immediately, while you are still on the course.

In that case, take out the CDL while you are on your course. As soon as the course is over, take out a personal loan at a much cheaper rate instead and pay back the CDL with it.

Other points to consider

- If your course is close enough to the job you already do, in terms of its scope, it may be possible to ask your employer to consider sponsoring you instead of taking out a loan.
- There are many loans that imply they are similar to CDLs. They may even offer a payment holiday for the duration of the course you want to study. But unlike a CDL, all unpaid interest is added to the loan. This means that the capital you owe at the end of the course is much bigger.
- If you want to do an MBA, your best bet is to ask your employer for help. Failing that, you can apply for a Business School Loan from NatWest. The scheme is backed by the Association of MBAs (www.mba.org.uk) and enables you to cover course fees and personal expenses.

TOP TIP

As long as you are still on your course, a CDL is effectively interest free. So if you are able not to touch the money it may be worth borrowing more from your CDL than you need, leaving the money untouched in a high interest savings account. You then pay the money back at the end of the course.

But be aware that since June 2008, rules on CDLs have changed: in order to prevent fraudsters who offer fake 'courses', pocket the money from student applicants and then disappear a few weeks later, grants may be paid in instalments. This may make it more difficult for you to earn as much interest from such a scheme.

Credit rating and how it works

Being turned down for credit is, simultaneously, one of the most humiliating and annoying experiences that can befall anyone.

When it happens, you are usually in a public place and your application to pay for an item in '12 easy instalments' has been rejected within earshot of anyone hanging around the till. Or the card company you went to for its wonderful new 12-month, 0 per cent deal on both balance transfers and new purchases 'regretfully' informs you that your request has been declined.

Inevitably, when something like this happens, you immediately tend to think that something has gone wrong at the other end of the application process. It must have been a technical mistake. Or the information held about you is wrong. Or they have the wrong person altogether.

Of course, any one of these explanations may be true. But it is equally possible that the company that turned you down had the correct information. And the information – maybe rightly – suggested that you were a bad risk.

But don't think the problem is unique to you: the Credit Card Research Group estimates that, depending on the issuer, between 40 and 60 per cent of all applications are turned down, often for reasons that seem hard to understand. In the wake of the current credit crunch, it is even more likely that you may be turned down for credit. So how can you overcome the problem?

First, it is important to understand how credit rating actually works.

How does credit scoring happen?

Before they agree to lend money, issue a new card, finance your hire-purchase deal or even agree whether to let you have a new mobile phone on contract, all providers go to one of three main credit reference agencies (Equifax, Experian and CallCredit) to find out more about you. These agencies collate a mass of publicly available information about every adult in the UK from a variety of sources, and lenders use that data as a large element of the scoring system they use when considering credit applications.

For example, this information includes:

- people on the electoral register at your address
- your credit agreements, including details of any late payments and defaults, which can be held for up to six years
- court judgements and bankruptcy orders against you – these are also held for six years
- previous applications for credit
- people living at the same address as you, such as your family or friends, plus information on their credit history

By the way, the reference agency itself is not the one doing the 'blacklisting'. It simply provides information to a credit provider. It is then up to the credit provider to operate its own scoring system based on the information it has received.

This means that depending on the individual criteria applied by a provider, you may either be accepted or turned down.

TOP TIP

Have you ever applied for a seemingly cheap loan, only to be offered one that is significantly more expensive than you imagined?

This is because the Office of Fair Trading (OFT), the credit watchdog, only requires companies to advertise a 'typical' APR. This means 66 per cent of loans offered by that lender must be the same as or less than the rate advertised.

Many observers have long wondered exactly what checks are carried out to ensure this actually is the case.

How to improve your credit rating

If you are turned down for credit, it is easy to get upset or to imagine that nothing can be done about it. In fact, there are many things you can do. Here are five tips that can help.

1 Check that the information held on you is accurate
The Data Protection Act entitles you to know what is in your credit report and, where necessary, challenge its accuracy.

If you want to do this, send your name and address, together with a cheque or postal order for £2 and a list of your previous addresses over the last six years, to each of the agencies at:

CallCredit: Consumer Services Team, PO Box 491, Leeds, LS3 1WZ
Equifax: Credit File Advice Centre, PO Box 1140, Bradford, BD1 5US
Experian, Consumer Help Service, PO Box 8000, Nottingham, NG51 5GX

2 Correct any inaccuracies

If there is a mistake on your file, you cannot simply ask for it to be corrected by the reference agency itself. You must contact the organisation that provided the information. The reference agency can help with details, including an address.

Then write to that organisation and ask it to correct any incorrect details about you and to inform the credit reference agencies. You will have to provide a written reason, with a factual explanation, for that organisation to correct any wrong or misleading information about you.

For example, if there are entries that involve credit account information (lenders or credit card issuers for example), you must contact the lender directly. Depending on what needs correcting, here is what you can do.

- If the credit reference agency is unwilling to change information about you because it is 'factually based', you may add a 200-word statement to your credit file, to explain any entry on it. This is called a Notice of Correction.

    If you add a Notice of Correction to your credit file, any organisation checking your credit file will have access to this – and lenders searching a database for information held about you are obliged to read your Notice of Correction.

    This may slow down their decision of whether to offer you the product or service you have applied for.
- If for some reason you have failed to pay a bill, the organisation you owed money to may have gone to a County Court (a Sheriff's Court in Scotland) and obtained judgement against you, ordering you to pay.

This is known as a County Court Judgment (CCJ), or a Decree in Scotland. You do not have to be there when it happens and the first you may know about it is when a court notice drops through the letterbox, especially if you did not receive notice of the court hearing, perhaps because you have changed address. But details of that CCJ will be on your credit file.

If you have paid off that debt, contact the County Court directly and ask for a 'certificate of satisfaction' to the effect that you have paid the debt concerned.

■ If there are entries on your personal file that relate to a family member, partner or someone else living at your address and you have had a financial relationship with them in the past, you need to have a 'disassociation' created. This breaks the link between you and anyone else at the address who may have a poor credit history.

3 Pay off and reduce your bills and debts

There are simple – and perhaps obvious – rules to follow.

■ Pay ALL your bills on time. Late payments can have a negative impact on your rating.
■ If you have missed payments, get up to date. The more you pay your bills on time, the better your rating.
■ If you are having trouble making ends meet, contact your creditors or see a credit counsellor. The Citizens Advice service in your area will help. This may not improve your credit rating immediately, but if you can begin to manage your credit and pay *something* on time, your rating will get better over time.
■ Pay off debt rather than move it around. It may seem clever constantly to shift your debt between 0 per cent credit cards, but sooner or later it will catch up with you.

Note that although unpaid credit and CCJs remain on your file for six years, they will be marked as settled once you pay the debt. This could be taken into account and work in your favour when making future applications.

4 Build a credit history

Ironically, one of the reasons why many people get turned down for credit is that they lead blameless financial lives.

There is nothing lenders or credit card issuers like better than a good credit record, where borrowers show they can successfully repay amounts they owe and manage credit and debt. But maybe you don't borrow money; you pay your bills on time, don't use a credit card and only have one bank account.

This means that when a credit check is carried out, there's nothing there for a credit provider to see whether you would be a good or a bad credit risk – so you get rejected.

How do you deal with this? Here are a few tips.

- Apply for a small overdraft on your account, maybe even a small loan. Pay it back religiously.
- Lenders check the electoral roll to confirm your name and address, so make sure you are registered to vote with your local authority.
- One or two successful credit card applications could be seen as a sign of credit-worthiness. You may want to apply for one just for that reason.
- Conversely, bear in mind that every time you apply for credit it leaves a 'footprint' in your file which will be seen by other lenders and issuers. A large number of searches over a

short period could signal over-commitment or even fraud, so you may think it sensible not to apply until absolutely necessary. One option when applying for credit is to aim for a lender where you stand a better chance of not being rejected. Some price comparison websites, like Moneysupermarket, will do a free check – without creating a footprint – and tell you who your likeliest credit provider is.

5 Be honest when you apply for credit
If you've moved a lot in the last three years, don't be tempted to leave out any previous addresses. This could be seen as an attempt to conceal unpaid credit at that address and treated as suspicious.

Also, be honest about your credit history. If you've been in difficulties in the past and been unable to meet your repayments, or you've got CCJs, make sure you tell your prospective lender.

Finally
If you have a poor credit history, it can seem as if you will never be able to get back on the side of the angels and obtain the credit most of us need to make life that little bit simpler.

The reality is that things are never that bad. It may take time, but anyone who is determined to do so can repair their credit history – and keep it clean.

Credit cards

Credit cards, as anyone who has ever had one will know, are both fantastically useful and deadly dangerous. They're like a wood chisel: if you know what you are doing, it's a wonderful and effective tool. If you don't, a slip can lead to serious damage, either to yourself or whatever you are carving with it.

What are their benefits? You've probably got a card already, but here are some of them:

- **convenience:** they allow you to buy what you want, when you want it, subject only to you not breaching your credit limit. A small piece of plastic gives you access to purchases in many tens of thousands of shops worldwide;
- **interest-free credit:** this is frequently overdone. In reality you will rarely get the 56 days or so that are often advertised. After all, your purchases within a given month are added together. But the fact that you can defer payments by some days is always useful;
- **track your spending:** though you may not spend much time looking at it, every statement you receive tells you what you spent that month. It could even turn into a useful budgeting tool;
- **rewards:** many cards offer bonuses when you use them, ranging from reward points to cashback deals, which essentially means you are being given a discount on what you buy. Some cards offer insurance cover on new purchases;
- **protection against fraudsters:** a little-known feature of the Consumer Credit Act means if you make a purchase worth between £100 and £25,000 with a credit card, you are protected if the item is faulty or, if purchased online, does not arrive. Subject to some conditions, your card issuer will give you a refund and chase up the money from the person you gave your card details to.

The potential disadvantage of cards is now well known too. The fact that all you need to do to make a purchase is hand over a card, or key in a few digits on an Internet page, makes the act of spending money strangely impersonal – and far too easy at times. After all, it's not like having a handful of cash: when it's gone, you have nothing left to spend.

It is easy to go from there to not being able to control how much you spend. Crucially, therefore, it is worth looking at a few important points that can help you get the best out of your credit card.

How many cards do you need?

At the last count, there were more than 67.5 million credit cards in circulation in the UK. Strip out the millions of people who don't have a card at all and those who might only have one and it's easy to see that the majority of people will have at least two or three, sometimes many more than that.

The reason is simple: people take out a card for a special reason, perhaps because they saw it offering a good deal at the time. But when that deal ends, they rarely use it again.

Should you do the same? No, especially if you don't intend to use the card again. It's much better in such cases to cut it up and send a nice letter to the card provider cancelling that card.

Quite apart from relieving yourself of the temptation to make use of all those cards at some point, the total amount of credit you have available is carefully noted in your records, held by credit reference agencies.

This means it is available not just to other card companies but mortgage lenders, mobile phone suppliers and so on. They can see how much you are allowed to borrow overall, whether you do make use of it or not. In turn, this could restrict its availability when you really need it.

75

That's not to say you shouldn't have more than one card for different types of spending. But each one has to 'justify' its place in your wallet or purse. So what cards should you have? The following list is a highly subjective one and may not satisfy everyone's needs. But in my book, you need just three:

- **a reward card:** this is the card to use regularly. Probably the best card to have is the one that offers the highest spending cashback or a similar reward. American Express, for example, pays you back 5 per cent in the first three months and 1.5 per cent thereafter – great for Christmas. Be ruthless: you might prefer Sky's card, which cuts £1 off your Sky bill for every £100 spent. But you would still save more on Sky bills if you paid them with the Amex card;

- **a holiday card:** this is only for when you go travelling. The reason you need one is that every time you use your credit card while you are abroad, you pay a minimum of 2.75 per cent in transaction charges. Only a handful of cards do not levy this fee and they include the Post Office;

- **a balance transfer card:** if you have a raft of debts, it may make sense to transfer them to a single card, typically one charging 0 per cent for up to a year or longer plus a fee – on balance transfers. Keeping this card separate matters a lot. Many 0 per cent cards might charge no interest on a balance transfer, but they do on new spending. And they operate a 'payment hierarchy' whereby all payments are used to pay off your cheap or 0 per cent debts first, leaving your new purchases to rack up interest. So take out this card. Transfer your debts to it and set up a standing order to pay them off. But then cut it up so you can't use it ever again.

TOP TIP

Are there exceptions to these three cards? Sometimes an offer comes along that is too good to pass up: a year or two ago my girlfriend and I were admiring some furniture in Marks & Spencer. The store offered 0 per cent interest for two years for the first purchase on its credit card.

I used the card to buy two sofas and two armchairs for £2,400 and then set up a standing order to pay M&S back £100 a month. During that time, the card was never used on any other purchase. A standard loan would have added at least £150 to £200 to the cost of that purchase.

Similarly, if you were in the market for a new car, General Motors offers discounts based on points built up using its GM card. So it may pay to identify something you really want, see if there is a card that lets you have it at a discount and then use that one.

What to watch out for when applying for a card

It is a fact that all cards are NOT created equal. This applies not only to the amount of interest they charge but to a host of other terms and conditions, even the timing of that interest. So what kind of things should you watch out for?

- **The APR.** This stands for Annual Percentage Rate. It tells you the interest rate you must pay based on a period of a year. Generally, the lower the APR, the better the card for you – but not always, as will be explained later.
- **Late payments and exceeding the personal limit.** Most of us are likely to do this at some stage or another. As long as it only happens once in while, it is relatively unimportant. But if you get into the habit of not paying on time, it does matter.

The good news is that since 2006, late payment charges have been capped at £12 a time by the financial watchdog, the Office of Fair Trading. The bad news is that you could still pay heavily if you exceed your personal limit. For example, simply going £5 over the limit could leave you with a £12 charge. In some cases, exceeding the limit could invalidate a 0 per cent interest deal on a card, leaving you to pay the full APR.

By the way, just because you think you have plenty of time to pay doesn't mean this is so. The clock actually starts ticking when a statement is issued, not when it reaches you and, mysteriously, that can take up to seven or eight days.

It then takes up to five working days for the cheque to arrive and be entered into the issuer's system, plus a further three to five days to clear. The solution is simple: use a regular monthly direct debit to pay your bills on time.

■ **Using a card abroad.** We've touched on this one already. But there is a further point to note: every time you withdraw cash from an ATM while abroad, you will be paying an average of about £4 in charges.

You also face a higher rate of interest on that portion of your overall card debt, with some card companies charging up to 30 per cent APR on cash withdrawals – and if the 'payment hierarchy' places expensive debt at the bottom of the pile, that cash withdrawal could cost you a lot of money.

■ **How interest is charged.** A few years ago a committee of MPs asked a Cambridge University mathematician, Dr Robert Hunt, to work out the annual interest rate on a credit card deal.

After spending the best part of an afternoon with a calculator and a wet flannel round his head, Dr Hunt managed to work out one set of charges. But he admitted that it would probably take him a lot longer to do the same with all the other methods used by credit card companies.

In April 2007, the consumer group *Which?* filed a so-called 'super-complaint' with the Office of Fair Trading, claiming that there were at least 12 different ways in which interest was calculated by the UK's top 20 credit card providers in the UK. Between them, these providers control 90 per cent of the credit card market.

Which? identified six features, other than interest rate, that determine the cost of credit:

1 **interest-free periods:** whether an interest-free period is offered or not and, if so, whether it is conditional on the balance from the previous month being paid off in full;

2 **end of interest charge:** whether interest is charged until the date of repayment in full or until the statement date before the cardholder repays the balance in full

3 **interest calculation:** whether interest is calculated by multiplying the average daily balance in the month by the monthly rate or as a sum of the daily balances in the month multiplied by the daily rate;

4 **start of interest charge:** whether interest starts being charged from the date a purchase is made or the date it is posted to the account;

5 **statement day:** whether interest is charged until the day before a statement is produced, or until the day on which the statement is produced;

6 **interest on interest:** whether the interest-bearing balance in the current statement period includes interest charged on the previous month's statement.

The consumer group then looked at how these different factors impacted on the charges that people pay, taking four cards as an example.

Over a year, a credit cardholder spends £500 on the 15th of each month. They repay on the 10th and their repayments follow a four-month repayment cycle:

- in the first month they repay £180
- in the second they repay £180
- in the third they repay in full
- in the fourth they repay in full

Over the year the cardholder would end up paying off very different amounts of interest, depending on which credit card they own:

HOW CREDIT CHARGES SHAPE UP	APR	Annual cost
HSBC MasterCard	15.9 per cent	£58
Sainsbury's Bank MasterCard	15.9 per cent	£83*
American Express Nectar	12.9 per cent	£68*
Lloyds TSB Advance	11.9 per cent	£71**

* This card charges interest from the statement date up to when the cardholder repays in full. The interest-free period for new purchases only applies if the previous month's balance is cleared in full.
** This card has a lower APR, but no interest-free period for new purchases.

Source: *Which?*, April 2007.

Note: cards quoted and rates charged may no longer be available

Store cards

Say you are window shopping one Saturday, you like the look of something and want to buy it. Unfortunately, it's a week until payday, your bank account is running on empty and your credit card is maxed out. What do you do?

For many people, the answer would appear to be a store card, of which there are more than 11 million in circulation, with some £2 billion of credit outstanding on them at any one time.

Store cards are another form of credit offered by individual shops or chains of shops. They are often available at the point of purchase and can be used immediately, subject to an often-perfunctory credit check.

The beauty of such a card in the scenario above is that you could, in theory, go right ahead and buy what you want. So, should you take one out?

The consensus among financial experts is that you should avoid them like the plague. The simple reason is that they are very bad for your financial health – to the tune of at least £55m a year.

This, at least, was the finding of the Competition Commission, a watchdog which checks to ensure that the market works effectively, following a two-year investigation published in 2006. The Commission concluded that the annual percentage rates on the cards were on average 10–20 per cent higher than they needed to be. With few exceptions, APRs on most store cards are clustered around 30 per cent, much higher than rates on many credit cards. This is far more than is needed to cover providers' costs and make a reasonable profit.

Two honourable exceptions include the John Lewis card and, slightly surprisingly, one from IKEA.

Why do store cards cost so much?

- Store cards are often sold as a way of getting cheap offers on goods rather than on the basis of their APRs. Most people apply for a store card because there is a one-off 10 per cent discount, or similar, available for applicants that day.
- Customers do not understand the cost of buying insurance policies, such as payment protection insurance, which are often bundled into the cost of the card.
- Card statements do not provide enough information about the charges being levied.

In many cases, the way store card providers make their profits is extremely cynical, using late payment fees which contribute up to 20 per cent of gross revenues. Frequently, they also add store card insurance cover in the event of illness or accidents (payment protection insurance or PPI). Up to 32 per cent of policyholders have this cover – even when they don't need it.

So what should you do?

Simple: if you took out a store card because of a special discount available at the time, cut it up and throw away the pieces. Pay off what you owe and start again.

Another easy thing to do is simply to switch your store card debt to any 0 per cent credit card, or even one charging less than 16 per cent APR, of which there are many.

A third option you may want to consider is a fixed loan for, say, one year. Rates are now as low as 5–6 per cent APR. Meanwhile, you may well appreciate the 'discipline' involved in making regular monthly payments to bring down your overall debt level.

But whatever you do, cut up that store card.

The loans maze

If it hasn't done so already, there will come a time when you really want something very expensive but don't have enough money to pay for it outright. That's when a loan comes in handy.

At its simplest, a loan is a sum of money you borrow and pay back over an agreed period of time at a rate of interest that is usually fixed in advance.

But things are never quite that simple, of course, so here are a few things that you need to know about loans.

The first is that there are, in fact, two main varieties: secured and unsecured loans.

Secured loans: this is a form of credit that is 'secured' against something, usually your property – assuming you own one – and very occasionally a car.

The deal here is that as long as you make regular payments, as agreed at the outset, there is no problem. The advantage of a secured loan is that, because you are offering up 'collateral' in the event of non-payment, the rate of interest you will be charged is likely to be significantly lower than for an unsecured loan.

However, the downside is that if you were to miss one or more payments, your home is potentially at risk and there is the possibility of it being repossessed.

If you are just starting out, though, the chances are that you won't come across a secured loan. This is because it requires both that you own a property (or at least have a mortgage on one), and that it is worth significantly more than the mortgage for any loan to be advanced to you on it.

Probably, therefore, you will go for an unsecured loan.

Unsecured loans: here, the lender simply charges you a rate over a given period, typically between one and five years although both shorter and longer loan periods are available.

Although the rate of interest may be somewhat higher than for a secured loan, your home is not at risk if you don't pay it back.

That said, failure to pay will definitely harm your credit rating, plus there is the possibility of the lender taking you to a County Court. If it obtains a judgement against you, bailiffs could be sent in to take possession of items to the value of your debt.

What to look for in a loan

If you are applying for a loan, here are some things to ask about.

The Annual Percentage Rate (APR). Lenders are likely to have less leeway in deciding how they apply APR than they do with credit cards, simply because loans involve fixed payments for fixed periods of time.

However, do make sure you ask the prospective loan provider to tell you the monthly repayments over a given period – and how much interest you will be expected to pay.

Redemption fees. Borrowers who want to pay off their loans early often face redemption penalties of up to one month's interest.

Moreover, different lenders operate various rules. Most will insist that the interest penalty is the same regardless of either the amount repaid or the period still left.

So if you take out a three-year loan, the interest penalty is the same regardless of whether it is paid one month into the loan, or one month before it was due to run its course.

Not all lenders do this. So always ask how much the redemption fee is – and how they calculate it.

Since 2005, changes to the Consumer Credit Act have been made to ensure consumers get a fairer deal:

- the lender cannot charge more than 28 days penalty interest on a loan that is being repaid early;
- lenders must now calculate the actual amount of saving a customer makes by repaying early;
- when customers take out the loan they must be shown the amount payable at quarter, half and three quarters of the way through the loan. This can be the exact figure or a representative amount based on how much per £100 or £1,000. Be sure to find out how much this might be.

Loan insurance. Often, if you ask for a quote on a loan, the lender will automatically add on the monthly cost of loan protection, so-called PPI cover.

Many lenders won't even tell you they are doing this. So if you sign on the dotted line, you may end up with cover you do not want or need.

It gets worse. Not only is PPI cover expensive, but many lenders add the full cost of the insurance itself to the loan at the outset, leaving customers to pay interest on the cover AS WELL AS the sum they borrow. This is why it can add up to 30 per cent or more to the cost of the loan.

You should therefore be aware that:

- if you redeem a loan early, you could end up paying an interest penalty not just on the loan itself, but also on the cost of the PPI cover;
- if you are repaying your loan early and PPI was sold as part of that loan, then its cost must also be factored into any early repayment quote. If it was sold as a separate contract then it must be calculated separately.

It is worth noting here that the issue of PPI has attracted a great deal of attention by various financial watchdogs and the competition authorities.

There has been repeated evidence of mis-selling of PPI cover in recent years, with many insurers and lenders being fined millions of pounds for this. In November 2008, the Competition Commission published a report suggesting that insurers and loan providers should be banned from selling PPI for at least 14 days after the loan has been offered.

If you really need protection, it can make far more sense to buy the cover separately from an independent broker. It is not only cheaper, but you face a smaller redemption penalty.

Daily or monthly interest? Most lenders charge interest on a monthly basis. In other words, the payment you make is only credited towards the capital sum owed once a month. This makes a big difference to total interest costs, especially to those who pay off their loan more quickly. Ideally, you should look for a lender that charges interest on a daily basis.

Pressure selling. Many people who already have a loan may still find themselves in growing debt. They will often be offered the chance to 'consolidate' that debt by taking out a new loan that includes the money to pay off the old one, plus whatever else they need.

This is generally a bad step to take.

- You will end up 'wasting' your old loan insurance, assuming you had any.
- You will have to pay redemption penalties on the old loan. They tend to get added to the new loan, increasing the amount you owe.
- If you are in a position where you can't afford to pay off the old loan, it is unlikely that you will be able to do so with the new one.

Contacts and links

MoneyMadeClear: www.moneymadeclear.fsa.gov.uk

Insolvency Helpline: www.insolvencyhelpline.co.uk

Consumer Credit Counselling Service: www.cccs.co.uk

Citizens Advice: www.citizensadvice.org.uk

National Debtline: www.nationaldebtline.co.uk

Office of Fair Trading: www.oft.gov.uk

Buying your own home

Had this book had been written three or four years ago, it is almost certain that it would have strongly recommended that you get your first step on the housing ladder as soon as possible.

It is a measure of how times have changed in the past 12 months or so that an argument like this can no longer be made safely. Indeed, if you are a recent graduate, the idea buying your own property in the next year or two seems both ludicrous and unattainable.

Perhaps the best way of deciding whether this is a financial area to get involved in is to look at the pros and cons of buying a home.

Why it does *not* make sense to buy

- **Why burden yourself with extra debt?** The chances are that, having just completed several years at university, you may already owe thousands of pounds to your bank and credit card issuer, the Student Loans Company and quite possibly your parents.

- **Why buy a depreciating asset?** House prices have been falling sharply since the end of 2007 and it is hard to see them recovering soon. They fell by about 15 per cent in the course of 2008 and most predictions suggest they may drop by a similar amount in 2009 and possibly a similar amount in 2010.

- **It is a ball and chain at a time when you least need it.** Buying can tie you down when you want to move on, for example if your career requires you to move elsewhere in the UK, or you just fancy taking time off and going abroad for a while.

89

There is also the danger of 'negative equity'. If the value of your home falls below the level you paid for it – and especially the amount you have borrowed to buy it – selling a property becomes impossible unless you make up any difference between the sale price and what you owe your lender.

- **Mortgages are difficult to come by.** Mortgage lenders – once so willing to offer huge loans to almost anyone – are now much tougher on first-time buyers. The best mortgage deals are now available only to those with big deposits of at least 20 per cent or more.

  In any event, forget about being able to borrow mortgages worth six or seven times your income. Today lenders are far more likely to restrict lending to a traditional 'multiple' of three to four times earnings.

- **Ownership costs more than you think.** First there is stamp duty to consider: this is a tax of 1 per cent on all purchases over £175,000 until September 2009. It rises to 3 per cent on purchases over £250,000 and is payable on the entire sale price.

  In addition, experts suggest that unless you are living in a new-build property, you should look to set aside 1 per cent of its original asking price every year on basic repairs and upgrades. This expense is cumulative: if you don't spend it this year, you will need to do so next year.

Why it *may* make sense to buy

There are several reasons why it is still worth considering a home purchase – if not immediately, certainly in the coming year or two.

- **Property prices rise on a historical basis.** It is important to understand the difference between 'cyclical' falls, such as those ones experienced in the mid-1970s and early 1990s and the long-term movement in prices, which tends to rise over much longer periods of time.

For example, according to Nationwide Building Society, the average house price was £10,388 in the first quarter of 1975. Even after price falls of 14.6 per cent in the past 12 months, according to the Nationwide index, average prices in October 2008 still stood at £158,872.

- **You may miss out on the 'bottom'.** Many would-be buyers think they can simply wait until prices reach their lowest ebb and buy a property then. Some may be able to do that. But most will almost certainly not recognise that point and miss out on some of that recovery.

  For example, in the autumn of 1994, after the last property market correction, prices rose by almost 9 per cent in the following nine months. Yet this gain was missed by most buyers, who stayed out of the market until the evidence before their eyes was incontrovertible. Why not negotiate a large reduction in price today to take into account where you expect the market to be in 12 months' time?

- **Negative equity is not always as frightening as you may think.** It mostly becomes a problem if you cannot afford to keep paying the mortgage (perhaps because you have borrowed too much), or if you want to sell up and move elsewhere but don't have the money to meet the difference between what you owe your lender and the lower price you'll get if you sell up.

  But in reality, you will have paid up to 10 per cent of the capital owed on a mortgage within five years. Assuming you also paid a 10 per cent deposit on the property, that's a 20 per cent buffer after five years.

- **Mortgages are not impossible to find.** Yes, they are much tougher to obtain than before, but if you are determined to climb up the housing ladder and have a deposit available, it's not out of the question. It may also be possible to get some help from your parents or to buy jointly with a friend.

- **Demographics are on your side.** In 2006–2007, the last available figures, the government estimated that there were some 200,000 homes added to UK housing stock, a huge increase on 'normal' trends, which are closer to 150,000 a year.

  The government wants 200,000 homes to be built a year, rising to 240,000 a year by 2016. This is to take into account the expected number of new households, growing at about 220,000 a year. But in 2008, it is estimated that barely 100,000 will be built and as few as 65,000 in 2009. That creates pent-up demand – which means prices are unlikely to keep falling forever.

- **You can be your own master (or mistress).** If you want lime-green walls with cerise curtains, rubber flooring, a genuine avocado-colour bathroom suite and a black parachute hanging over your water bed, you may have to own the property they go into!

Home buying rules

Regardless of when – or whether – you decide to buy, there are three key rules you should bear in mind when buying a property.

1 Do not treat property as an investment but as a roof over your head. Regardless of whether it rises or falls in value over the next few years, it is your home first and foremost.

2 Only buy something you really like. Part of the reason why people feel hard done by if prices fall is that they always treated it as a stepping stone to somewhere better, rather than somewhere they would love living in, no matter what happened to its price.

3 Only buy what you can realistically afford. Your mortgage payments should be no more than 30 per cent of your net monthly take-home pay. This ensures there is enough left over to pay your other bills, as well as having a reasonable buffer to meet any potential interest rate increases.

Types of mortgage

Until the end of 2007, there were an estimated 16,000 different mortgages available to UK borrowers. One year later, that number had fallen to barely 3,500 as the credit crunch forced lenders to restrict lending significantly.

That said, there are still mortgages available for determined first-time buyers. Here are the most common types.

Standard variable rate (SVR). This rate can move up or down, depending on the cost of borrowing money for the lender. These costs are loosely linked to the three-month London Inter-Bank Borrowing Rate, or Libor, which is the rate at which banks lend money to each other.

Fixed. This rate is pegged at a certain level for periods, generally between two and five years, although both shorter and longer fixed periods are available. The advantage of a fixed-rate loan is that it allows borrowers to know months, even years, in advance what their monthly payments will be. This makes budgeting easier.

Discount. A discounted mortgage is similar to variable loan deals, in that it can move up or down in line with base rates. The difference is that the discount is pegged to a rate that is below the variable mortgage rate. Discounted mortgages run for periods ranging between six months and five years, although most on offer are one- to three-year deals.

Tracker. A tracker mortgage is linked to the base rate set by a central bank, almost always the Bank of England. It is usually pegged at a certain percentage rate above base. Lenders can and do change the level at which a tracker is set. They also set 'collars', a level below which they will not cut mortgage payments no matter what happens to the base rate.

What to look out for in a mortgage

Application fees. Only two or three years ago, a typical mortgage fee was about £300. Today, it can be up to £800 or more. Some of the cheapest deals will actually charge a percentage of the loan, up to 2 or 3 per cent. Such deals are not generally suitable for first-time buyers and usually only worthwhile if the amount you are borrowing is extremely high.

Annual or daily interest calculations. In the former case your capital repayments, and therefore the interest you must pay on the sum still outstanding, is calculated every year.

With daily interest, each capital payment instantly reduces the amount you owe – and therefore the interest payable.

Compulsory insurance. Sometimes a particularly cheap deal is available only if you take out home and contents cover or even life insurance with the lender. Some experts have suggested compulsory home and contents cover can add the equivalent of 0.35 per cent to the cost of a deal.

Mortgage payment protection insurance (MPPI). This covers you against accident, sickness and unemployment. Again, this is offered by lenders in order to protect your mortgage payments to them.

The cost is usually about £5.50–£6.00 for every £100 of monthly repayments. For example, a 25-year £100,000 mortgage at a 6 per cent interest rate would mean monthly MPPI payments of £38.50.

By shopping around independently, you can find very similar cover for about £3.50 per £100 of monthly payments, a saving of about £15 – or £4,500 over the lifetime of your loan.

Redemption penalty periods. If you switch your mortgage to another lender during the lifetime of a special deal, or for a stipulated period after it ends, you may have to pay a penalty.

Depending on how attractive the original offer was and how far into the redemption period it is, this can be anything up to six months' interest. Look for offers without redemption penalties, or ones that only apply for the period of the deal itself.

BUYING COSTS

When you're buying a property there are a range of expenses you will have to meet, both before and after a purchase. Here are the main ones.

Surveyor's valuation fees. On a typical first-time buyer's home, this will be about £300. If the property is old or you are not too sure of its condition, it may be better to have a full survey rather than a simple valuation. This can cost upwards of £500 – £600.

Lender's application/completion fee. This used to cost about £400, but in the past few months, the cost has moved to about £800 for a reasonably good deal. The fee is usually levied at completion and is generally added to the cost of the mortgage itself.

Mortgage broker's fee. A broker can be useful for a first-time buyer, in that he or she should know the market well and can probably source a mortgage for you more easily than you could do yourself.

But the broker's fee can be up to 1 per cent of the mortgage amount – although typically, the final amount payable is cut back to about £500. Some brokers charge a lot less, or are even "free" – but then put pressure on you to take out other policies with them. If in doubt, say no.

Solicitors' fees. These can be up to £600, plus so-called 'disbursements', the costs incurred by solicitors in carrying out their work which they will re-charge to their clients, such as photocopying, postage, couriers and also local searches and Land Registry fees.

Stamp duty. This is a tax levied by the government on all property purchases. The rates are set out below:

Property value	Duty payable
£0 to £175,000 (until 2 September 2009)	0 per cent
£175,001 to £250,000	1 per cent
£250,001 to £500,000	3 per cent
£500,001 or more	4 per cent

BUYING YOUR OWN HOME

Note that stamp duty applies to the entire amount you are paying on the property, not just the element above the particular thresholds. For example, a £250,001 home will cost £7,500.03 in stamp duty.

After the purchase, here are some more expenses that you will have to pay.

Council tax. This is a tax to pay for local council services, such as rubbish collection, education and policing. Taxes are banded according to the value of a property, with a typical Band D annual charge of about £1,300.

Banding is based on property valuations of more than 10 years ago, unless your home is newly built, in which case you will pay more, based on recent valuations.

Insurance. Home insurance is compulsory and will pay out if your home is damaged or destroyed. Contents insurance is for your belongings within the home. The total cost of both is usually about £500 a year.

Life insurance. A life insurance policy will pay out in the event of your death or that of your partner. It can cost about £30 a month for a 25-year policy that will pay £100,000 in the event of a 35-year-old's death.

Utility bills. Gas, electricity, water and phone bills can cost up to £1,000 a year or more for a first-time buyer, assuming a typical two-bedroom property.

Repairs and maintenance. Factor in roughly about 5 per cent of your monthly mortgage payments to pay for the upkeep of your property.

Ground rent. If you live in a flat and are a leaseholder, this is a fee you have to pay to the freeholder as a condition of your lease. It's usually a small amount, such as £50 or £100 a year.

Buying at auction

When people find it increasingly difficult to sell a property, they resort to auctions. The advantage of an auction is that as long as the reserve price is low enough, sellers are guaranteed to find a buyer for their home within a few minutes.

For buyers, there are both advantages and disadvantages. Here are some of them.

Pros

- You don't have to deal with pushy estate agents.
- It's just you against other buyers.
- The sale is legally binding. Vendors can't change their minds.
- It's incredibly quick: you can end up owning a property within 28 days, having exchanged contracts days earlier.
- You could end up with a bargain. In September 2008, the average price of the 3,993 homes sold at auction between June and August was 23 per cent lower than the same period a year earlier. The price drop was far greater than for properties sold through estate agents – today's bargain at tomorrow's lower prices.

Cons

- It can be a daunting experience.
- Sometimes, the pre-auction period is not long enough to carry out in-depth checks on the property.
- You can't change your mind once you have won the bidding.
- The temptation is to pay too much because people get carried away by the atmosphere of the auction itself.
- Unless you have lined up a loan and a lawyer who can expedite everything in double-quick time after the auction ends, you could be in trouble.
- You could end up with an expensive wreck.

If you are buying at auction, here are the basic rules to follow.

- Always attend a few auctions just to see what they are like. Soak up the atmosphere and get a sense of how the bidding works and the ways people compete.
- Contact all auction houses selling properties in the areas you're interested in and ask for their catalogues. Some will have the details online, so be prepared to do a few searches.
- View one or more properties.
- Ask yourself why the property is being sold at auction. It could be that the seller wants to get rid of it quickly. It could also be that the property is unsellable by other means.
- Unless you can spot things like damp, poor wiring, dry rot, subsidence and a myriad other major structural problems that may affect the property, pay for a surveyor to go round and prepare a report for you. This is particularly important if you are later hoping to persuade a lender to offer you a mortgage on it.

- At the very least, take round a skilled builder who can give you an idea of how much it will cost to bring the property to the right standard. Then add a few thousand pounds.

Buying with others

Buying a property together with friends has both pluses and minuses. It can be a fantastic way of increasing your purchasing power and landing somewhere much nicer than you might have been able to afford on your own, especially in the current climate, where mortgages are hard to obtain.

The advantages of buying your first home with friends include:

- you get more value for your money, effectively moving two rungs up the ladder in one go;
- you share the cost of the deposit, purchasing fees, ongoing mortgage repayments and household bills.

On the minus side, there is a danger that while you were good friends when going to the pub or on holiday, you might not be compatible as housemates.

The kinds of things that really tear households apart are:

- noise
- privacy
- tidiness
- borrowing personal possessions
- equitable sharing of bills
- bringing other friends or partners home

There will also be costs of a legal agreement between yourself and your friend(s), plus you may need to take out life insurance to cover your side of the mortgage if anything happens to you.

You need to agree:

- how much each of you will put in as a deposit
- how legal and other purchase costs will be met
- how you'll pay the bills, including the mortgage, insurance and utilities
- who takes responsibility for cleaning and keeping the place tidy

In practice, this means a co-habitation agreement, where issues are thrashed out and all parties sign legal documents in which specific reference is made to each of these points.

You also need to discuss what happens if one person needs to move out and/or sell up and the other one does not. It is not unheard of one friend to sell their share of a property to the other housemate, but bear in mind that the buyer could be left with a stamp duty bill.

If you buy someone else's share in the property for more than £175,000, you will be liable for 1 per cent of that amount in tax, the current stamp duty level. Above £250,000, the amount you would have to pay in stamp duty rises to 3 per cent, or £7,500.

Legal forms of home ownership

If you are buying jointly with someone else, make sure that the purchase contract sets out the right form of joint ownership.

There are two main types.

1   **Joint tenancy.** Under this version, neither party can sell their share of the property without
    the other's agreement. If one party dies, the other automatically inherits his or her share.
    This is suitable for adults buying a property as a couple, but less so if you are buying with
    a friend.

2   **Tenancy-in-common.** Under the terms of this arrangement, each party can sell on his or her
    share, either while still alive or through a will. This is much more suitable for friends buying a
    property together when they don't intend to live together as a couple.

You may want to insert something in the personal contractual agreement
with the other party whereby you agree that you each give the other first
refusal on your share of the property and how the price for that share will
be determined.

Protecting your mortgage payments

For many mortgage borrowers, making sure their monthly bills are paid
regardless of whether they fall ill or become unemployed is vital,
particularly in the current economic crisis.

There are two key things you need to do protect yourself if you fall ill.

1   Check what contractual sickness benefits you are likely to receive from your employer. Many will
    pay some or all of your wages for a minimum period if you are ill. At the very least, you are
    entitled to Statutory Sick Pay (SSP). This is paid at a fixed rate of £75.40 a week from 6 April
    2008 for a period of up to 28 weeks.

2 Consider a mortgage protection insurance policy. These are available through mortgage lenders or separately from specialist insurers. Typically, a policy may cost about £5–£6 for every £100 of monthly mortgage payments it protects against. So a £500 monthly mortgage could cost up to £30 a month to protect. However, specialist insurers are generally significantly cheaper than lenders, so it always pays to shop around.

Many mortgage protection policies also cover against unemployment, although most operate stringent rules that govern how long a policy must have been in force before you are allowed to claim (this is to prevent so-called 'adverse selection' by people who know they are likely to lose their jobs).

Also, you may face a long waiting period after you become unemployed until you can claim, while payments may only be made for a year or two. In most cases, this should be enough until you get back on your feet.

Mortgage interest support

Faced with increasing numbers of people whose homes are at risk because they cannot pay their lenders, the government decided to revamp its rules to provide more help for homeowners. These came into effect after January 2009.

■ If you are receiving income support, income-based jobseeker's allowance, or income-related employment and support allowance, you will now be entitled to support on your mortgage interest payments (not the capital) after 13 weeks. Previously the waiting time was 39 weeks for new claims, or in some cases 26 weeks.

- Before January 2009, it was only possible to claim help with interest payments on loans up to the value of £100,000, or the first £100,000 of a larger loan. That level has now been increased to £200,000. The rate at which interest can be paid will be fixed at 6.08 per cent until June 2009, when new rates will be decided.

Note that there are strict eligibility criteria. For example, if you are out of work but your partner is still in a job, the amount paid towards your mortgage interest will depend on his or her earnings.

Whatever your situation, if you find yourself in financial difficulties, one of the first things you should do is contact your mortgage lender and work with them to find ways of ensuring you can stay in your home until you find new work or, if you have been ill, are able to resume your job.

Money and bankruptcy

Ten or 20 years ago, the notion that someone in their 20s, fresh out of college and just starting work, might consider going bankrupt would have been laughed at.

Today, it is no longer treated as a joke. According to surveys, up to 10 per cent of all graduates have considered bankruptcy as a way of avoiding having to pay back their student debts.

Up until 2004, this was actually feasible: a loophole in the law meant it was possible to declare oneself bankrupt and avoid having to pay back one's student loans. In the space of a less than a year, upwards of 1,000 graduates went bankrupt.

However, the government has plugged that particular hole and student loans will still need to be paid off even if you are declared bankrupt. Moreover, there is still a lot of moral stigma against going down that route.

But even so, you may be facing a lot of other debts and the notion of simply declaring yourself bankrupt is appealing. So what does it involve and what are the consequences?

New laws mean that, for some at least, going bankrupt has become an easier option, with the penalties for taking such a radical step being reduced in a number of cases.

What is bankruptcy?

At its most basic, bankruptcy is one way of dealing with debts you cannot pay. Bankruptcy proceedings aim to do the following:

- free you from overwhelming debts so you can make a fresh start, subject to some restrictions;
- make sure your assets are shared out fairly among your creditors.

How to become bankrupt

Although a decision to go bankrupt can be difficult to make, the act itself is remarkably easy. Bankruptcy petitions (or 'sequestrations' in Scotland) are usually presented either at the High Court in London or a County Court near to where you live or trade. A similar procedure applies in Northern Ireland. In Scotland, you have to go through a Sheriff's Court, which will order that both debts and assets of a person should transfer to an appointed trustee.

Your local court will give you the name, address and telephone number of the nearest County Court that deals with bankruptcy.

How soon are you discharged from bankruptcy?

Changes to bankruptcy laws allow a first-time bankrupt to be discharged from their debts and released from restrictions after a maximum of 12 months. And where cases are administered quickly and creditors agree, this period can be reduced. This applies to bankrupts who have failed 'through no fault of their own' and who co-operate with the authorities.

That said, 'dishonest, reckless or blameworthy' bankrupts could face restrictions for up to 15 years. Bankruptcy Restriction Orders (BROs) will bar people from obtaining credit without disclosing their status, trading under a different name or holding a company directorship for between two and 15 years.

The Insolvency Service will decide, on a case-by-case basis, if a BRO should be pursued through the courts.

Drawbacks of bankruptcy

Despite the alleged easing of rules concerning bankruptcy, there remain important disadvantages to this course of action. They include:

- you may still lose any assets of real value, including your home, vehicle, investment policies, life insurance and possibly some pension entitlements (if it is deemed you paid excessive contributions to avoid that money being handed over to your creditors). You might be able to keep your vehicle if you can prove you can't do your job without it;

- while you are bankrupt, any assets you acquire – such as inheritances or insurance settlements – will be lost. And, yes, it does include any wins on the Lottery (apparently that's the question almost every bankrupt asks their insolvency examiner). If your bankruptcy was deemed to be 'dishonest, reckless or blameworthy', this period may be extended for up to 15 years;

- your building society, landlord and all other creditors will be informed immediately. All your bank accounts will be frozen, credit cards taken away, some HP agreements will be ended and many of your worldly possessions taken away and sold;

- if or when your bank unfreezes your accounts, you'll find that you won't be allowed a chequebook or an overdraft. You will also find it difficult to open a new bank account elsewhere;

- you cannot obtain more than a total of £500 of credit without declaring that you are an undischarged bankrupt. To do so is a criminal offence;

- you may lose your job and will certainly not be able to practise in some professional areas, including accountancy and the law;

- you CAN be self-employed, but you will have to declare the name in which you were made bankrupt on your business correspondence and records so that people running credit checks on your business will be able to find out your full financial history. You may also be required to provide regular accounts to your trustee.

Individual voluntary arrangement (IVA)

If bankruptcy is not the solution, what is? One alternative option is an individual voluntary arrangement, or IVA.

This is an agreement to pay back a certain amount of money to creditors, though not the full amount owed, at a set rate each month, over a certain period of years.

At the end of that time, the debt is judged to have been settled in full.

For people burdened with heavy debts, IVAs have several advantages:

- you may only pay back a percentage of your debts;

- you only have to make one monthly payment or, in some cases, a one-off lump sum;

- the IVA is legally binding so that your creditors cannot change their minds once they have agreed;

- you are able to operate a 'normal' bank account as long as it does not have an overdraft facility;
- it may safeguard your property – although creditors will almost certainly require savings and realisable assets (endowment policies, premium bonds, ISAs) to be cashed in;
- it does not affect the ability to hold public office or your professional status.

How does an IVA work?

Once you decide an IVA is right for you, you contact an insolvency practitioner, or IP, who will do the negotiating with creditors on your behalf.

The trade body is the Association of Business Recovery Professionals, or R3, as it likes to call itself. It has lists of members in each region and can be contacted via its website.

The process works as follows.

- Your IP will ask you questions about your current financial situation. Based on the information you have given, a repayment amount will be agreed with you.
- Once proposals have been drawn up, you check and sign them and return to your IP.
- He or she then makes an application to a court for an Interim Order which states that you are working to achieve an IVA.
- Once this is in place, no creditors can take legal action against you. A creditor meeting is then arranged, which you should attend. In the case of a consumer IVA, creditors or their representatives rarely attend the meeting as most prefer to vote by fax or by post.

- For an IVA to be approved, creditors vote either for or against the arrangement. If creditors vote for the IVA, it will be approved. If creditors don't vote, it is assumed that they are in favour of the IVA.
- However, if just one creditor votes against the IVA and he or she represents less than 25 per cent of your total debt, the meeting is suspended until a later date and other creditors who did not vote will be called upon for their vote.
- If the creditor who voted against the IVA represents more than 25 per cent of the total debt you owe, the IVA fails. This is because IVA can only ever be approved if 75 per cent in monetary value is voted for.

Most IVAs are generally based around a regular monthly payment over a period of 60 months. As long as you keep up the repayments, when the term of your agreement is finished, you will be free from these debts regardless of how much has been paid off.

During the period of your arrangement, your financial situation is reviewed regularly to see if there has been any change in your circumstances.

The rules in Scotland – Trust Deeds

Scottish law is slightly different. There, what happens is that you have a Trust Deed. This is a legally binding agreement between an individual who is unable to pay his/her creditors and a licensed Insolvency Practitioner (the trustee).

The trustee puts together a form of proposals to the creditors for approval and, if agreed, then administers the Trust Deed.

Provided certain conditions are met, the Trust Deed may be registered as 'protected', preventing creditors from taking further steps – such as sequestration (the Scottish term for bankruptcy) – to recover debts due to them.

Who pays for the IVA?

When you are paying out a fixed sum each month, it may feel that you are paying nothing to the insolvency practitioner.

In fact, he or she is taking a cut of your monthly payments, with this sum generally hidden from you.

Ultimately, the insolvency practitioner is getting a cut of what he or she is able to deliver to creditors. A typical fee may be up to 15 or 20 per cent of your monthly payments.

The potential downside of IVAs

Many debtors tend to see IVAs as a soft touch, certainly before they apply for one. If so, they may be in for a rude awakening.

In order for an insolvency specialist to get all creditors to agree to the IVA, he has to promise to extract the maximum possible amount from you.

Bear in mind that, at the end of the day the amount of money he or she gets is dependent on how much you pay.

In addition, many IPs are dealing with the same creditors – banks, credit card issuers, HP firms and so on – on a regular basis. To maintain their trust in the process, IPs can't be seen to be slacking off in terms of how much you are asked to repay.

This helps to explain why many people who take on IVAs find that they are being clobbered anyway, and why some of them move on to bankruptcy proceedings after a year or two – although many of them have simply not been able to rein in their old spending habits.

Administration Orders

If you have a number of small debts (maximum £5,000), you can apply to the court for an Administration Order.

This means that you pay the court one regular amount you can afford and they distribute it to the creditors on your behalf, although a small charge is made.

While an Administration Order is in force, creditors must stop badgering you and are obliged to accept the payments made via the court office.

If you pay your Administration Order instalments regularly, the court may agree to write off any remaining debts after three years, giving you a fresh start.

To qualify for an Administration Order, you must have at least two debts and one of the debts must be a county or high court judgement and your total debts must not be more than £5,000.

PART III

Saving

10 Saving money

This section of the book aims to discuss some of the arguments about why it makes sense to save your money and how to do it.

Frankly, with anything affected by two of human beings' most powerful emotions – fear and greed – there is a whole range of issues to address that go beyond the mere 'mechanics' of where to stick any spare dosh. In addition, the very public experience of the past two or three years is that many so-called experts have been exceptionally bad at investing our money. The current crisis is partly the result of us trusting them too much.

So it makes sense to look at the subject in more detail and see whether there are any lessons to be learned and, if so, how to apply them.

Why bother saving?

Actually, it may seem perverse to talk about saving and investing if you are only in your 20s. After all, you probably left college recently and are still burdened by massive debts incurred when you were a student.

Meanwhile, your wages are almost certain to be low, barely enough for a couple of rounds or to buy some new clothes every now and then. How on earth can anyone manage to save money on your income? Besides, isn't this is a time to be having fun, not sticking money in a bank or worrying about a pension?

And anyway, the lessons of the past year or two have hardly been great for investors, have they? In 2008 alone, world stock markets collapsed by anything up to 75 per cent in some cases, although the UK's main share index fell by a far more 'modest' 32 per cent. In the process, the retirement dreams of millions of people, possibly including your mum and dad or your grandparents, have been hard hit.

Under such circumstances, it's hardly surprising that many people – possibly even you – decide they would rather spend the money they earn and worry about the future when and if it comes.

So why should you bother saving any money? Here are three important reasons.

1 You are almost certain to need a nest-egg sooner rather than later.
Some people assume that the only reason for saving is because at some distant point in the future – maybe as far away as 40 or 50 years' time – they will need a pot of money when they stop working. That time feels so far away, it hardly seems worth worrying about.

We'll come back to that point in a minute, but it is important to realise that you'll probably need to access a lot of money far sooner than that, probably within five to 10 years.

The fact is, a key consequence of the financial crunch is that it has changed the landscape completely when it comes to obtaining credit – and credit is what we have all made ample use of in recent years. But from now on, it won't be there; you'll have to put cash upfront if you really want something.

Let's say you want to buy a flat or house at some stage in the next few years. The problem is that whereas a year or two ago it was relatively easy to obtain a loan worth 100 per cent of a property's asking price (with some lenders willing to advance even more), today you'll be hard pushed to find anyone prepared to offer more than 90 per cent.

That means having to put down a deposit of at least 10 per cent of the property's price. Even then, the chances are that any mortgage deal will be expensive. Put simply, the smaller your deposit, the higher the interest rate charged.

Once upon a time, some young people might have made use of the 'Bank of Mum & Dad' to raise that extra cash. This involved their parents increasing their own mortgages and handing over the money to help finance their kids' first home purchase.

But falling property prices and the unwillingness of banks to lend money even to well-off adults have largely put paid to that tactic. Besides, your parents may well be worrying about their jobs and paying off their mortgage – which means you are more likely to be on your own.

So even with today's falling prices – and assuming you don't live in London or the South East of England, where prices are higher – you may well need around £15,000 to £20,000 to finance a property purchase in the next few years.

And even if you decide not to buy a home but to rent instead, don't imagine this is an issue that simply affects first-time buyers. The same logic also applies to other types of loans: lenders are less willing to offer easy credit for almost anything, from car purchases to credit cards to buying a settee. One way or another, you will need to be ready for a big cash hit in the next 10 years.

2 Saving for retirement does matter, actually. So here you are, enjoying yourself, getting off your face every weekend, going on great holidays and having the time of your life – which makes you totally unlike some of the sad old wrinklies queuing up at the supermarket with their baskets of special offer dog food, or waiting at the bus stop and heading for home just as you're getting ready for a top night out.

Leaving aside the fact that they were probably like you 50 years ago and had much the same attitudes to life as you do now, the main reason why they wear shabby clothes and buy cheap food is that they haven't got enough money to afford better.

In other words, because they weren't able to save more, they now find themselves economising all the time.

The fact is, not only is it tough having to scrimp day in, day out, but the amount of years you may have to spend doing it is growing all the time. We are all living longer and your life expectancy after you retire will probably be several years greater than it is for today's pensioners.

Unless you start to prepare for that now, the chances are it will be you queuing at some future supermarket counter, with the basket of cheap dog food.

3 Saving actually works. Many young people worry that the amount they can realistically save is so puny that it hardly seems worthwhile.

However, one of the chief beauties of saving is that growth in the amount you tuck away is actually accelerated by something called 'compounding'. This means interest is gradually added not just to any monthly amount you set aside, but also to the interest already there.

Sounds complicated? Let's look at it in a very simplistic way. Say you put £1,000 into a savings account and the interest on it is 5 per cent a year.

After 12 months, your savings will be worth £1,050. After two years, that sum is now worth £1,102.50, because interest at 5 per cent was added not just to the original £1,000 but also the £50 interest accrued in the first year. And so on.

At this stage it still doesn't sound much, but after 30 years that initial £1,000 would be worth £4321.94, with interest making up a massive £3,291.40 of that amount, even if you never added another penny to the original lump sum. Try working it out with any sum at www.link42.co.uk.

Of course, in reality things can be much more complicated. The chances are that you would be saving a monthly amount, not just a one-off lump sum. That monthly amount may go up or down, depending on how much you can afford at any one time. Interest rates are also likely to fluctuate, as they have done recently.

Most importantly, inflation eats away at the value of any savings: if annual inflation were 2 per cent throughout the previous example's 30-year time frame, then the 'true' value of that lump sum would only be around £2,510 at today's prices.

We'll talk more about inflation later. But the important thing to note here is that saving even a seemingly insignificant amount now can have a huge impact on the final value of your lump sum when you are likely to need it in many years' time.

In effect, £10 a month saved today is the equivalent of saving £20 or £25 a month if you start in 15 years' time. Put like that, doesn't it make more sense to sacrifice a little now rather than pay out a lot more later?

Nine key savings rules

Before we get on to where to stash your money, there are nine vital rules you should always follow when saving. Here they are:

- **Don't try to save if you have massive debts.** Any interest you will earn is highly unlikely to be higher than what you owe on, say, a credit card charging a typical rate of interest of at least 15.9 per cent APR, a bank overdraft and even many loans (apart from a Student Loan). So it makes sense to pay off your high-interest debts first.
- **Decide what you are saving for.** Any savings will almost certainly have several aims at once: some short-term goals (for example a holiday or a car next year); a medium-term one (a deposit on a home in 10 years' time); a long-term one (retirement).

   This helps you focus on what you are doing. It will also help determine where you save your money and how much risk to take with your investment. It may also mean that you need to have several 'pots' for your money, each of which is for a different goal.
- **Think about an emergency fund.** You never know when disaster might strike: a sudden illness or an accident; being made redundant; your car or computer packing up just when

you need them most. Most experts suggest you should have at least two or three months' worth of after-tax income set aside to meet any emergencies if they arise.

In practice, this well-meaning advice is probably unrealistic for someone in their 20s: if you can manage it, great. If not, be prepared to use your other 'short-term funds' as and when necessary.

- **Be clear about your attitude towards risk.** There's no point in investing in shares if you are likely to constantly worry that their price will tumble in the short and medium term. Share prices are volatile and can both rise and fall *sharply* for years at a time – although they do historically deliver better returns than standard savings accounts over longer time periods of 15 years or more.

  Equally, if you are in your 20s and saving for, say, your retirement, you should consider higher-risk investments as there is more time for them to match any falls with a subsequent rise.

- **Spread your investments.** This may seem obvious, but many people think purely in terms of buying individual shares they think might do well or even one or two funds. The problem with this approach is that if that share or fund nosedives, they risk losing a lot of money.

  The key to reducing volatility and not losing money is to diversify your investments as much as possible (more on this subject later).

- **Get advice.** There are very few people competent enough to handle their own saving and investment strategy from beginning to end. This means everyone needs at least one of two people to help, possibly both of them: an independent financial adviser (IFA) and a fund manager.

  The IFA is someone who can talk to you about all your needs and suggest an overall investment strategy to meet them. This should include a selection of funds or similar products that take into account your goals and risk profile. The fund manager is a specialist when it comes to buying equities. He or she will actually invest money channelled to him (or her) by the adviser into a range of shares or similar.

■ **Think about charges and fees.** Most people who invest tend to think that performance is the key to the returns they receive. They are right, of course. But there is another factor to consider: investment charges. This is the amount you pay to have your money looked after and comes in two parts – an initial investment charge, which can be up to 5 per cent of the funds you invest, as well as an annual charge of around 1.5 per cent of the funds under management.

The truth is that most funds, with few exceptions, tend to deliver similar performance over time. This in turn means charges can have a disproportionate impact on the overall returns you will receive. Remember: a 2 per cent annual charge over 25 years means your total fund will be worth 25 per cent less than one charging 1 per cent and delivering the same performance.

TOP TIP

When looking at a fund's charges, don't just focus on its management fee. Look out for its 'total expense ratio', or TER. This includes not only the manager's annual charge, but also costs for other services paid for by the fund, such as the fees paid to the trustee (or depositary), custodian, auditors and registrar, as well as any marketing costs. These typically add another 0.5 per cent to a fund's annual costs, but in some cases have been known to double the management fee itself. All funds are now required to tell you their TERs.

■ **If it sounds too good to be true, it almost always is.** This is a truism, but it's amazing how many people get caught. According to the government's own figures, up to 28 million people are targeted each year and an estimated £1bn is lost to fraudsters.

Many of these scams simply promise better-than-average returns. The fact is, if such a strategy were successful, you can be sure that its merits would be widely discussed everywhere and lots of people would be urged to pile in. The fact that this isn't happening should tell you something: the reality is there are no best-kept secrets to investing, no magical potions or unique strategies that someone hasn't tried before. If in doubt, always check out a firm's credentials first with the UK financial regulator, the Financial Services Authority.

■ **Keep an eye on your investments.** Just because your savings or investment decision may have been sound at the time it was made does not necessarily mean it is valid for all time. This means if you opened a savings account, check it every six months to a year to make sure the rate you are being paid is among the best. If you are investing in shares or in a fund that itself invests in shares, talk to your adviser at least once a year to make sure the factors that determined your original decision still hold true today.

How to invest

It may seem obvious, but if you want to set money aside, one of the most important things you need to work out is why you are bothering to save at all.

The issue has already been touched upon earlier in this chapter, but there is little point to saving unless you have a fairly defined target in mind for all this money. From a psychological point of view, goals matter: studies show people are much more motivated to save if they know what their nest-egg will eventually be used for.

For example, financial providers offering savings products aimed at parents with kids know they are highly unlikely to see them cashed in early. Why? Because wanting your child to have a good start in life makes you much more likely to put money aside than simply doing it as a whim.

In addition, any saving goal involves a time frame of some sort. Given that you have a finite amount of money you can afford to save each month, you need to work out how long you intend to spend achieving a particular objective. For example, a deposit on a house probably involves a five- to 10-year investment period. Setting aside money for retirement means you are looking 30, maybe even 40, years further out.

These time frames not only help define your investment strategy, they may also require different financial products, each with a variety of tax implications and benefits.

Although everyone's various reasons for wanting to save money can't be slotted neatly into particular boxes, we can try to set some basic ground rules. Here are some ideas of what you should do if you are saving for the short, medium and long term.

Short-term savings

This is an easy one. For a start, if you are going to put money aside for anything between a couple of years to four or five, the one thing you don't have to bother with is any type of equity-based investment. Shares are too volatile to dabble with over short periods of time. Although returns can sometimes be amazing (in the four-year period between April 2003 and April 2007, the FTSE 100 index of leading UK shares rocketed about 60 per cent), prices can also fall like a stone, as we saw more recently. Looking at the same index, by January 2009 the FTSE 100 was only about

12 per cent above its level in April 2003, which means overall returns averaged barely 2 per cent a year.

So, if shares don't cut it, where should you put your money?

High-interest savings accounts are almost certainly the best place to go. The way to find one is to go to one of the many price comparison websites and look for the best rate payable on regular savings accounts.

Another very safe place for your money is National Savings & Investments (NS&I), the government-backed savings institution. The fact that it is linked to the government means your money is reckoned to be ultra-secure, or at least as safe as it ever can be in the current climate.

NS&I offers a range of tax-free saving schemes, often for fixed periods of up to five years. Some of them guarantee to pay above existing inflation rates, although these savings schemes tend to be adjusted up or down, depending on what happens to retail prices.

Overall, the rates paid by NS&I are not as high as you might be able to get elsewhere in the private sector. But many people are prepared to trade higher returns for greater safety – and at a time of potential bank collapses, who can blame them?

TAX-FREE ISA

If you are planning to save a lot of money in the short to medium term – and very little besides – you may want to think about putting your cash into an Individual Savings Account, or ISA.

These are so-called 'tax wrappers' (remember that term, as you'll come across it later) and money saved in one of them is free of income tax you would otherwise pay.

Each tax year, from 6 April to the following 5 April, you are entitled to save up to £3,600 in a so-called cash ISA. This can either be through lump sums or regular monthly payments.

In order to be eligible to open an ISA, you have to be aged over 18, a UK resident and this must be the only ISA you are opening. Providers give your details to HM Revenue & Customs, so you won't get away with more than one ISA.

TOP TIP

When looking for a savings account, unless you are able to lock away your money and forget about it, try to steer clear of those where the seemingly high rate of interest is paid by means of 'bonuses', or where there are excessive interest penalties for cash withdrawals.

Bonuses are used to make any interest payable look great: you might be offered 5 per cent, of which 3.5 per cent is the basic rate, plus an extra 1.5 per cent if you leave the money untouched for at least 12 months. In reality, many people find themselves needing some of their savings back from time to time, which makes the real rate of interest much less exciting.

Medium-term savings

Here the picture changes, depending on exactly how long your savings plans are likely to last for.

If you are looking at a five- to 10-year time frame, then the chances are that you would still probably be better to stick with savings accounts. At the end of the day, you really can't afford to risk losing a large chunk of your money because of stock market volatility. In which case, much the same rules apply as with shorter-term investments, but perhaps with a slightly greater emphasis on the tax-free aspect of savings. This is because although reducing the tax you pay is always important, it becomes much more so over longer periods of time.

Think about it: if you are saving regularly and are paying basic rate tax on your work-based income, you will also be liable to pay 20 per cent tax on any money stashed into your savings account. In fact, your bank will already be deducting it for you and paying interest on your money net of tax. Now, over a period of two or three years, that may not matter so much. Say you have stashed away £1,000 in that time, earning 5 per cent interest. That 20 per cent tax deduction will reduce the interest you receive by £10 over one year, which is hardly likely to kill you.

But multiply those savings over 10 years. The amount you have put together becomes a less modest £10,000, on which 5 per cent interest is accruing at a rate of £500 a year – and the taxman is now taking £100 a year. As you can see, sheltering your savings in an ISA now makes even more sense. And if you think you're likely to be saving for at least 10 or 15 years – in other words, your time frame is stretching beyond the medium and into the long term – the argument in favour of equity-based investments becomes even greater.

By the way, ISA savings allowances are offered on a 'use it or lose it' basis: if you don't use up your annual £3,600 cash ISA allowance in the relevant tax year, you can't get it back the following year. And if you withdraw money from an ISA, you can't top it up again in the same tax-free environment.

But here's another good point about ISAs: you can also use them to hold shares. In fact, you can hold up to £7,200 in a normal ISA in total, of which up to £3,600 can be saved in cash with one provider. The remainder of the £7,200 can be invested in stocks and shares with either the same or a different provider. So once your time frame begins to move outwards, think about using the second element of your ISA allowance for shares.

Long-term savings

This is where potentially you have the widest range of options, not just in terms of what you invest in but also the 'vehicles' you can invest in.

Shares

As we've already seen, one of the most noticeable things about shares is their volatility. One of the more surprising statistics is that in early January 2009, the FTSE 100 index of leading companies stood at more or less the same level it was at in mid-1997 – about 4,500 points. In other words, the argument goes, had you invested in shares you would probably be no better off over those 12 years. In fact, you would be worse off, as inflation would have eaten into the value of any original investment.

But in investment, as with everything else, statistics don't always tell the full truth. Every year, Barclays Bank publishes a highly respected document called the Equity-Gilt Study, an annual look at the relative performance of different 'assets' people might hold as investments.

According to the Barclays Equity-Gilt study, there is a 99 per cent probability of equities outperforming cash savings over a period as short as 18 years. In fact, equities outperformed cash in 75 per cent of consecutive five-year periods and 93 per cent per cent of 10-year periods, too.

It should be noted that there are, of course, different ways of looking at these statistics. For example, if cash outperformed shares three quarters of the time over consecutive five-year periods, investors in shares lost money 25 per cent of other five-year periods.

And indeed, we don't know by how much shares DID beat cash deposits in those five-year periods, which begs another question: is the risk involved worth the return? If you might only get an extra 2 per cent a year from investing in shares, as compared to a savings account, but risk losing 30 per cent of your money almost overnight, is that an acceptable risk?

To which the answer might be that over five years, it almost certainly isn't. But over 40 years, it might well be: that extra 2 per cent a year, spread over a much longer period of time, could be worth an extra 80 per cent in the total value of your deposits. If that were your retirement fund, it might make the difference between £10,000 a year and £18,000. It now makes more sense, doesn't it?

Another thing about shares is that they are not all the same. They come from companies in totally different sectors, such as supermarkets, technology, commodities or banking, each with their own risk profiles. They can be US-based or Taiwanese businesses or from many other countries, all of which have varied business cycles that don't necessarily rise or fall in line with each other.

This in turn means that most investment experts would strongly recommend, when building a portfolio of shares, that you aim to straddle as many of these sectors and geographical areas as possible to reduce overall risk. That way, if one sector hits the buffers, your investment's overall performance will suffer less than it might otherwise.

DIVIDEND MAGIC

If share prices are often so volatile, why do investment experts keep banging on about the need to buy them? One major reason is dividends, a twice-yearly payout made by many companies to their shareholders.

When a company makes a profit, it can use that money in two main ways: it can either re-invest it in the business, or it can be paid to the shareholders as a dividend, or a mixture of both. This is usually set as a fixed amount per share, so shareholders can work out how much of a dividend they are likely to receive based on the number of shares they own.

Dividends don't need to be treated as income and spent immediately. If re-invested, as they often are, they form a vitally important part of total returns for investors.

In January 2009, shares in the FTSE 100 were yielding an average 6 per cent. If this were to continue, you would actually be doubling your money in 12 years even if share prices didn't budge at all in that time. But most experts believe dividends will fall. Logically, if share prices plummet, the yield will look higher for a short while – but if the reason for the fall is poor company performance, dividends will inevitably be cut. Historically, they have tended to average around 3 per cent a year, although some companies do pay more.

Over longer periods, the gains from dividends make all the difference in terms of share price performance. Had you invested £100 in equities at the end of 1945 with dividends reinvested, that money would be worth £131,000 now. By contrast, £100 in a savings account would be worth only £5,789, according to the Barclays Equity-Gilt study.

Corporate bonds

Shares are not the only things you can invest in for the long term. Another common 'asset' is corporate bonds: these are effectively IOUs issued by companies looking to borrow money for set periods of time. In return for you lending it to them, they promise to pay a certain rate of interest each year until the bond matures.

Bonds are graded according to the creditworthiness of the company concerned. If a company is considered to have a very low risk of defaulting on its debt, the bond is classed as being a high investment grade. In turn, this means the rate of interest that company needs to pay to borrow money is lower than one considered to be more at risk of default.

Generally, but not always, bonds are classed as lower risk than shares, especially those from very large businesses where, even if profits might suffer in a bad year, the company itself is not considered to be at risk.

It is also worth noting that the price of a corporate bond can move up or down in the same way as shares do. This is because a bond paying a certain rate of interest that may have seemed ordinary a year or so ago will look more attractive if rates are falling sharply (as they did in early 2009), or less enticing if rates rise.

So people who want to achieve a particular income will pay more for a bond that pays that higher income.

Property

In the past few years, property has also become an increasingly attractive place for people's money. We are not talking about homes here, but commercial property: offices, factories, warehouses and suchlike.

The reason why such property is attractive is that, if the economy is booming, there is more likely to be a high demand for commercial space. Rents generally rise regularly and this in turn increases the value of the investment itself.

Until 2007, commercial property was seen as a relatively secure, if unglamorous, investment. But in the past 12 months, the value of property has fallen sharply – and investors have discovered a fundamental downside to it: it is very illiquid, which means you can't sell it very easily.

What types of investments are there?

If you are looking to invest money, you will have many choices. The two commonest ones are buying individual shares, usually from a stockbroker, or going for what is termed a 'collective investment', typically a fund such as a unit or investment trust.

Buying individual shares on your own behalf carries a massive risk and is not really advisable for anyone who does not know much about investment. There are stockbrokers who have the necessary knowledge and skills to do this for you. But they recommend that you should have a portfolio of at least a dozen shares, usually more. In each case, you would be expected to spend a minimum of £500 to £1,000 in an individual company's shares, largely because there are dealing costs involved and doing so for smaller parcels of stocks becomes less cost-effective.

This is why most people tend to opt for collective investment schemes instead. These allow you to capitalise on someone else's skills: they will have access to research material about hundreds of companies and the experience to trade day in and out, selling or buying as appropriate. Because they are looking after tens, sometimes many hundreds of millions of pounds, they will be able to diversify into scores of companies, reducing your investment risk.

So how do these funds work?

Unit trusts. These are funds where a manager buys shares of companies based on his or her fund's remit – pharmaceuticals, or commodities, or financial companies. When you invest in that unit trust, you receive 'units' at the then prevailing price.

These are created with your money, which means the number of units that can be created is potentially infinite. If the share price of the companies the manager has bought goes up, so does your unit price. The same can happen in reverse. When you decide to sell up, your units are cancelled.

Pros

Unit trusts are reasonably easy to understand. They do what they say on the tin.

Cons

If too many units are redeemed by investors, the fund manager has to sell assets owned by the trust to pay the money back. The shares most likely to be sold are the better ones that are easiest to dispose of in a hurry – which can be the most valuable ones.

Investment trusts. These, too, are funds where the manager is buying shares in companies on behalf of the trust. But investors are buying shares *in the trust*, not units. Like any company, the investment trust has a finite number of shares. This means that not only can the value of the assets held by the trust (the shares in other companies) go up and down, so can shares in the unit trust itself that you are investing in.

This can sometimes lead to a seemingly contradictory situation, where the value of a trust's assets goes up but negative sentiment about the trust itself means that its own share price falls. In most cases, the asset value of the trust's holdings will be greater than the combined worth of its shares. This is known as a 'discount to net asset value', or NAV.

Also, unlike a unit trust, investment trusts can 'gear up', investing money that they borrow and offering the potential for greater gains if the investment goes well.

Pros

If the trust's combined share price is lower than the value of the assets it holds – this is called 'discount to NAV' – it means that you are effectively buying £1 of assets for less than its true price. Also, trusts are allowed to borrow money and invest that too. This is called 'gearing' and offers the potential for your returns to be higher. Annual fees on most investment trusts are typically much cheaper than unit trusts.

Cons

They are complicated and not so easy to understand. The discount can actually get worse, which means you risk losing more money than just a fall in the underlying assets. Gearing is also a double-edged sword: if the manager makes the wrong decision you lose even more – your own money and the money he borrowed.

Your overall investment strategy

All investors, even the most experienced ones, worry about losing money.

Stock markets never move in a straight line, although they can appear to do so for years, lulling many inexperienced investors into believing that their only trajectory is an upwards one.

The experience of the period between 2000 and 2003, when share prices virtually halved, and 2007–2008, when much the same happened around the world, shows how naïve such a view actually is.

But if it is true that markets can move down as well as up – and sometimes sideways too – how do you deal with setbacks and what strategies are there to minimise risks?

Here are five ideas you need to bear in mind.

- **Diversify.** This has been discussed already. But many people still make the mistake of believing that because they are invested in several funds, they are spreading their risks more widely. In fact, this may not be the case at all: regardless of who the manager is, many funds will often invest not just in the same sector but in the same companies. So make sure you ask your adviser to recommend funds where the investment style of each manager is distinct – as well as complementary – to each other.

- **Don't stay out of the market.** It is always tempting to tell yourself that the market is not doing well right now and you'll wait until it recovers before investing. But if you believe shares offer better long-term potential than cash deposits, this could be a mistake.

  Timing the market is almost always a mistake: share price rallies tend to be sudden and highly unpredictable, with the greatest rises happening in just a few days. Research published in November 2008 by the investment group Fidelity, on the performance of the FTSE All-Share index over the past 20 years, found that investors who missed out on only the 10 best-performing days in the market would have ended up with a portfolio worth roughly 39 per cent less than one that had been fully invested throughout the period.

  Conversely, missing the 10 worst-performing days would have enhanced an investor's returns by 60 per cent. But would you – or anyone – have spotted any of those 10 days?

- **Pound-cost-average.** When markets are volatile most people don't like the idea of pumping large lump sums into shares that may fall suddenly the next day. One way round this is to invest smaller amounts more regularly. This is technically known as 'pound cost averaging'. It means that when a market is falling, you are buying more shares (or units) with the same money. The reverse applies when the market is rising.

    Over a period of 12 or 18 months, your money will have bought X units or shares at an average price of Y. When the shares rise in, say, 10 or 15 years' time, the gains you make will be based on that average, not the lowest or the highest point.

- **Review regularly.** This, too, has been mentioned. But one of the things many investors forget, particularly when their portfolio is rising in value, is that its overall profile is changing.

    For example, if you are trying to reduce risk by placing a certain proportion of your money in bonds and another in raw material/commodity funds, a sharp increase in the value of one will mean it will start skewing the overall portfolio in that direction.

    Sometimes there's nothing wrong with that: you might want to let your profits run a little longer, especially if you think a particular sector has more growth to come. But you should remember that nothing lasts forever and the overall 'shape' of your portfolio matters more, risk-wise, than a short-term gain. Most important, if you do opt to skew your holdings in one direction for a while, make sure it's a conscious decision, not an accidental one you may regret later. Taking your profits in a profitable area and placing some of that money elsewhere is a useful tactic.

- **Cut your losses.** One of the most common mistakes made by many investors is to keep on holding onto a share or a fund long after it has shown itself not to be doing well. Psychologists have found that when stock markets collapse, this can induce a sort of emotional paralysis: people hate having to make tough decisions when it really matters. Some may even 'redraw' the facts in such a way as to justify their inactivity. Although the general advice to investors is never to panic in the face of a downturn, there will be times when you should make considered and rational decisions – which may well involve selling up.

Contacts and links

Trustnet: for up-to-the-minute statistics on how funds are performing, go here: www.trustnet.com

Investment Management Association: has information on funds investing both in the UK and outside. www.investmentuk.org

Association of Investment Companies: www.investmentuk.org

Association of Private Client Investment Managers and Stockbrokers: www.apcims.co.uk

Compare and find a stockbroker: http:www.fool.co.uk/brokers/information/choosing-a-broker.aspx

Understanding investment risk: www.which.co.uk/advice/understanding-investment-risk

Lipper Fund Intelligence: a website which allows users to look at both fund performance and charges, using the more accurate and reliable 'total expense ratio'. www.lipperweb.com

Morningstar UK: another source of online fund-related information for investors. available at www.morningstar.co.uk

FT Fund Ratings: the *Financial Times'* rating system for funds, which assesses them on the basis of charges, performance, risk and individual assets held in the fund. http:fundratings.ft.com/fundratings

Citywire: a new twist on the fund rating system, which looks not so much at the fund itself but at the manager who looks after it. www.citywire.co.uk

Money and retirement

Although most of the investment basics discussed in previous chapters apply to how you plan for your retirement, there are specific rules and options for those planning to save for a pension that are worth looking at separately. So here goes.

The state pension

Let's be honest here: the whole point of this section is to scare you into doing something about your retirement. And the best way to do that is to tell you what you are likely to get off the state if you have not managed to save much, or anything towards your retirement.

Essentially, there are several elements to what you will receive, based on your total earnings, National Insurance contributions and any small amounts of savings you manage to cobble together between now and retirement. Below are the most important ones.

Basic state pension

■ State pensions are currently paid at 65 for men and 60 for women. Over a 10-year period starting on 6 April 2010, women's pension ages will gradually be raised to 65. This effectively means if you are female and reading this book, you are highly likely to have to wait for a state pension until *at least* 65.

- The state pension age for both men and women is then set to increase from 65 to 68 between 2024 and 2046, with each additional year being phased in over two consecutive years in each decade. Put simply, if you were born in, say 1986, your retirement age will be 68.
- Not everyone will receive the maximum. It is based on the number of 'qualifying years' you have paid or been treated as paying National Insurance contributions. Both sexes will need 30 qualifying years for their full state pension, with people receiving 1/30th of the full basic state pension for each qualifying year they have. So if, for example, you had 10 qualifying years, you would be entitled to 10/30ths of the full basic state pension.
- In 2008–2009 the full basic state pension was £90.70 a week for a single person and £145.05 a week for a couple. This is uprated in line with inflation, so assuming a future government does not abandon this pledge – as it has abandoned so many others – that's vaguely what you can expect to get when *you* retire.

State second pension (S2P)

Since April 2002, those who stop work can receive a new additional state second pension, or S2P, which is earnings-related. The way S2P is calculated is mind-numbingly difficult:

- it relates to the number of years you have been contracted into the S2P when you reach state pension age;
- payments are currently based on a proportion of your earnings each year between a 'lower earnings limit' and an 'upper earnings limit';
- after 2012, the way payments are calculated will change again. In practice, the aim will be to ensure payouts favour those on lower incomes – and even then, it won't be much. For

141

someone earning £19,500 and retiring last year, the S2P element of their pension would have been £13.50 a week.

Pension credit

Pension credit is the government's answer to an eternal conundrum: how to make sure some people are helped in retirement without giving out money to those who have plenty of savings and don't need an extra handout.

Essentially, it is a form of pension top-up, aimed at people who reach retirement age but do not have much of an income other than their basic state pension.

The new system still involves people receiving a basic state pension based on their years in work. On top of this they also receive a guaranteed income top-up, or GITU.

Key to the process is the fact that what you get is reduced in proportion to any savings you may have or any pension you receive. If you have modest savings, you won't lose benefits as a result. Instead of taking away every penny over a certain savings limit, you are 'taxed' at 40 per cent instead.

This is done by reducing the amount of your pension credit by 40 pence for every £1 of income between a full-rate state pension and the GITU level.

Those who have a lump sum will have their savings calculated as 'deemed income' at a rate of £1 a week for every £500 of capital above £6,000.

For example, someone with £10,000 in the bank would lose £8 a week in credit, 'deemed' as the income they might receive on the £4,000 bit of their pot. This is an assumed interest rate of over 10 per cent after tax.

How much is all this worth?

Clearly, there is no way of knowing how much will be paid in 30 or 40 years' time, or even if pension credit will be in place. However, you can definitely gauge future intent by looking at today's figures.

- Currently, the maximum weekly income from the state, including pension credit, is £124.05 if you are single or £189.35 for couples.
- For singles, if your income is more than £124.05 a week but less than around £174 a week, the maximum credit of £19.71 is reduced by 40p for every £1 of income.
- For couples, if your income is more than £189.35 per week but less than around £255 a week, the maximum savings credit of £26.13 is reduced by 40p for every £1.

The simplest way to find out what you might be eligible for is to ask for a state pension forecast, based on your past work history and your answers relating to future National Insurance contributions you expect to make.

You can fill in a form, called BR19, through The Pensions Service, either online or over the phone. Go to www.thepensionservice.gov.uk.

Other income options

If you've been following things so far, two essential points stand out.

1   The state will pay a very small pension.
2   Although you might get more help off the state, any extra payment you might receive
     will be reduced depending on other savings you have, including company or private pension
     schemes.

Which means that to really benefit from saving you need to set aside more money than you might have originally have thought of. If so, how should you go about it?

Occupational pension schemes

One of the distinguishing features of the UK pension system, compared with many others in the rest of Europe, is the widespread availability of company retirement schemes.

Although their availability has been severely dented in recent years by a combination of high costs and claims of inflexibility by employers offering them, up to 12 million people in the UK remain eligible for an additional company pension. Five million current pensioners receive a retirement income from a company scheme.

There are two main types of company scheme: a 'final salary' one or a 'money purchase' pension. Employees can pay up to 15 per cent of annual earnings into either, not including the company's own contribution.

Final salary

These schemes are also described as 'defined benefits', because what staff may receive is agreed at the outset.

1   Employees pay a fixed amount of their salary into the pension scheme every month.

2   At retirement, the pension they receive is based on their final salary and linked to their years of service with the company.

Final salary schemes are good for:

- staff, in that their contributions are fixed, while the employer guarantees any shortfall in their pensions;
- employees who may spend most or all of their careers with one employer. Promotion should mean their salary rises faster than inflation, boosting their pensions at retirement;
- employers – if stock markets are rising. They can take 'contribution holidays' and, in some cases, even raid their pension funds (subject to trustees' approval) if the fund is in surplus.

They are bad for:

- those who change jobs often. They are unable to accumulate enough years of service and have to start all over again with each employer;
- employers – if stock markets are falling. They have to fund the guaranteed pension out of their turnover, which means bills can rise exponentially. Also, new accounting rules mean under-funding becomes more evident.

Risks

Final salary schemes rely on a combination of future stock market returns and ongoing company contributions to meet their guarantees to those coming up to retirement. If your employer goes bust, your pension is protected by a special lifeboat fund paid for by contributions from other occupational schemes. But higher earners may not get back every penny.

Money purchase

These are also known as 'defined contributions', because the employer knows in advance how much it will pay into the fund.

1   Both employer and employee pay an agreed amount into a fund each month.

2   The money is invested in stocks and shares, as well as bonds and other assets. At retirement, the employee's pot of money is used to buy an 'annuity', an annual income for life.

Money purchase schemes are good for:

- companies, who can predict exactly how much they must pay per employee every year, rather than relying on the vagaries of the stock market;
- staff who switch jobs. They build up much more transparent retirement funds and sometimes have a greater choice over how their money is invested.

They are bad for:

- staff whose employers don't make generous contributions into their pension pots. Surveys show that most companies don't.

Risks

Investing in the stock market means the value of a pension fund suffers if markets fall.

146

Also, the fund is then used to buy an 'annuity', an income for life. But annuity values can rise and fall, depending on interest rates. Which means you end up with a bumper pension pot – but a low annuity. That said, there are ways round this, which you'll definitely find out about when you get close to retirement age!

Finding out about a company pension

You can find out more from your employer or else directly from the company that administers the pension scheme.

Details of who to contact should be included in a booklet obtainable from your personnel or human resources department. You should have been given a copy of this when you joined the scheme.

Topping up a company pension

If you belong to a company scheme, now or in the future, you may feel that as long as you make regular payments into it – and your bosses do the same – you will enjoy a decent income when you finally stop work.

The sad fact is that for all bar the minority of people who join an employer and retire from that job 40 years later, a company pension will probably not be enough to fund a comfortable retirement.

There are several reasons for this.

■ If you are a member of several final salary occupational schemes, each time you switch jobs your final pension is calculated on the basis of your years of service and your salary at the time you left.

147

Someone who spent 10 years working for a firm with a two-thirds of salary scheme and then left while still earning £15,000, will receive a pension just shy of £2,500. Not a lot of use if their final salary at retirement is £45,000. Each 'sliver' of occupational pension won't give them a combined pension worth two thirds of their final salary.

- If you are a member of a money-purchase pension fund, employers' contributions are made in addition to your own payments. But surveys suggest that many employers with these so-called 'defined contribution' schemes pay in less than their equivalents who offer staff a final salary pension. At the same time, employees themselves tend to pay the same as their counterparts in 'defined salary' ones. At the end of the day, their pensions will be smaller.
- Women suffer particular problems: they earn less, often take time off to have a family and are unable to contribute towards a pension. Their company pension schemes will pay out less at retirement.

The only way to overcome these potential problems is to increase contributions into a pension.

Ways of doing it

Inland Revenue rules stipulate that the maximum contribution that can be made into a company pension scheme is 15 per cent of annual salary. This can be done in one of two ways.

1 Additional voluntary contributions (AVC). Most payments into company schemes do not reach the maximum limit. However, by law all companies offering a pension scheme to their employees must also offer the facility to make additional contributions, even if they don't add more money themselves.

These are known, funnily enough, as 'additional voluntary contribution' (AVC) schemes.

These contributions can be used to buy 'added years' that are counted towards your retirement, in the case of some final salary schemes. For example, an additional contribution of 10 per cent of salary for a year might buy an extra year of service in a final salary scheme.

Alternatively – and more commonly – they are invested in a fund running alongside the main occupational scheme and are used to buy an annuity at retirement. You sometimes have a choice as to which fund your AVC contributions will go.

2 Free-standing additional voluntary contributions (FSAVC). On the other hand, it is also possible to set up 'free-standing AVCs', a private top-up scheme. The principle is the same as an AVC, except that you get to choose the pension fund your money will go into.

In addition, an FSAVC is 'portable': when you go to a new employer, you can continue making contributions into the FSAVC there – assuming the main scheme requires you to pay under the 15 per cent limit.

Which is better?

Generally, most experts recommend that – other than in exceptional circumstances – you should stick with a company AVC. This is because, almost always, the management fees of an AVC are cheaper than its private counterpart. In some cases, while not actually contributing to the AVC scheme directly, the employer will subsidise its management costs, sometimes paying for them altogether.

Management charges form an important element of any pension fund's total return. Two funds with identical performance but where one has an annual management charge that is just 0.5 per cent higher than the other will deliver a 10 per cent difference in the final payout after 20 years.

The freedom to choose your fund is often presented as a key reason to go for an FSAVC instead. Again, surveys in the past have tended to show that people who opt for FSAVCs don't choose 'adventurous' investment options: they tend to replicate the same asset mix as a company AVC.

That said, history also shows that in some cases companies have selected the wrong pension manager for their AVCs. For example, throughout the 1990s many employers chose Equitable Life to look after their staff's AVC money. Equitable Life was almost forced out of business in 2001 after it hit the financial buffers. AVC policyholders with that company have lost out.

TOP TIPS

If you ever become desperate to boost your pension, here are two tips that can help.

Salary sacrifice: *this is where you agree a reduced salary with your employer in exchange for extra pension contributions paid to an occupational pension scheme. This saves the employer having to pay National Insurance contributions (NICs) on the salary sacrificed.*

The advantage to you is that the extra contributions benefit from being able to take a tax-free lump sum at retirement. You also benefit from inflation proofing of your pension after retirement (usually up to a 5 per cent maximum).

Note, however, that a salary sacrifice will reduce your pensionable earnings for maximum retirement benefits, your death in service benefits (such as life cover) and widow's pension.

Stakeholder pensions: under current rules, you are allowed to set up a separate stakeholder pension scheme and contribute into it – in addition to your employer's pension – as long as you have another source of income in that tax year, no matter how small.

For example, a properly constituted Saturday job, no matter that you only worked there for a couple of weeks, could be classed as a separate employment, entitling you to make an annual contribution of up to £3,600 into a stakeholder pension.

In fact, you would actually be paying in £2,880, because the Inland Revenue chips in the other £720 at 22 pence in the pound. Higher-rate taxpayers can then reclaim an additional 20 per cent, or £720, on their tax returns, reducing their effective contribution to £2,160.

Pension accounts

From 2012, the government is planning yet another change in the way people save for retirement by launching a new pension account into which everyone – both employers and their staff – will be required to save throughout their working lives.

The way it will work is as follows.

■ Employees will contribute 4 per cent of any earnings between £5,000 and £33,500 a year.

- Employers will make minimum matching contributions of 3 per cent on the same band of earnings.

- A further 1 per cent will come from the government in the form of tax relief. The money will be invested and the final pot used to buy a retirement income, just as with personal and money-purchase occupational pensions today.

- Employees will be given a choice of funds – including a range of ethical investments – but those who do not want to make a decision will have their contributions automatically paid into a low-cost default fund.

- The maximum annual contribution into the National Pension Saving Scheme (NPSS) will be £3,600. This limit will increase in line with earnings each year, so should effectively remain constant.

- The government hopes this scheme will operate with charges of just 0.3 per cent a year in the long run, much cheaper than the amounts typically charged for a personal pension.

- Employers will be allowed to phase in the new scheme. They have to contribute only 1 per cent to staff pensions in 2012, rising to 2 per cent in 2013 and 3 per cent in 2014.

- The money invested will be centrally administered, with all employees over the age of 22 automatically enrolled into the scheme, although they will be allowed to opt out.

The new scheme has not yet been officially launched at the time of writing. When it is, should you opt out of it?

The simple answer is no. There have been concerns raised about people in their 40s and 50s who may be caught in the savings trap outlined earlier: if you build up a pot that is not large enough, you will be penalised by missing out on an element of the state's own pension payments.

But for someone in his or her 20s, there is no way of knowing what kind of pension will be paid by the state in 40 years' time. So saving as much as you can today makes sense.

Plus, the opportunity to benefit from a matching contribution from your employer – effectively doubling the value of anything you put in – not to mention the state's own tax relief, makes this a no-brainer as a saving option.

Personal pensions

Another way to save more is through personal pensions. Although much maligned in recent years, they remain an essential part of long-term retirement planning.

What are personal pensions?

In essence, they are private 'money purchase-style' savings schemes, where money is paid into a fund which is then invested. The proceeds are used to buy an annuity (a regular income) at retirement.

- Payments can be made either monthly or by means of a lump sum, usually at the end of a tax year.
- Contributions, as we shall see, are based on a series of limits determined by Her Majesty's Revenue & Customs (HMRC).
- The investor, possibly in conjunction with an adviser, has a choice of assets into which his or her money should go.
- Retirement will be allowed at any age between 55 and 75, although the earlier an annuity is bought, the smaller it will be (because it has to be paid out for a longer period).

Some people can take their pensions earlier than age 50. For example, cricketers can retire at 40, as can divers, speedway racers and golfers. National Hunt jockeys and footballers can quit at 35 – flat jockeys need to wait until they are 45. Trapeze artists only have to hang on until they are 40.

Benefits and downsides of personal pensions

The advantages of a personal pension are significant.

- **Tax relief on the way in.** So keen is the government to help us save, that it offers extremely generous tax concessions to those who pay into personal pensions. For every £100 paid into one, basic rate taxpayers only have to contribute £80. HMRC chips in the remaining £20.

    The position for higher-rate taxpayers is even better: they not only receive the same tax relief, but can also claim back an additional 20p for every pound of contributions when they fill in their tax forms. Or else, they can offset this rebate against other earnings.

    Money inside a pension fund rolls up free of tax.

- **Partial tax relief on the way out.** When a personal pension is finally cashed in, a policyholder has the option – though not the obligation – to take up to 25 per cent per cent of the final lump sum as tax-free cash. This includes the taxman's own contribution as well.

Is there a downside? Well, there are three main ones.

1. **Tax.** The income you receive from a pension is taxed. Then again, most higher-rate taxpayers (bar the most wealthy) revert to the basic rate after retirement, making pensions a very tax-efficient vehicle.

2 **Time limits.** Annuities have to be bought with the pension pot by the age of 75. This can mean that if the annuitant dies shortly after taking out an annuity, his or her estate may not receive a penny of that pension pot. Again, there are ways round the issue and many companies can advise you accordingly.

3 **Lack of access.** With other types of investments you can access those funds in an emergency if you need to. But a pension is locked until you are 50 (soon to become 55).

Contributions limits

Since 2006, the government has changed the way in which you are allowed to make payments into a personal pension.

Essentially, you can save up to the equivalent of your gross income, up to the following levels:

- 2008–2009: £235,000
- 2009–2010: £245,000
- 2010–2011: £255,000

However, you will only receive full tax relief up to your current income. For example, if you earn £30,000 you will receive full tax relief if you contribute £30,000. You are able to contribute more than your salary but you will not receive tax relief.

If you do not have an income you can still contribute up to £2,880 net (£3,600 gross) per annum and receive basic rate tax relief of 20 per cent.

In the year before you take your benefits there is no maximum contribution limit.

Lifetime allowance

There is a maximum fund value you can have in your pension plan:

Tax year	Standard lifetime allowance
2006–2007	£1.50m
2007–2008	£1.60m
2008–2009	£1.65m
2009–2010	£1.75m
2010–2011	£1.80m

If your fund value exceeds this limit, a tax charge of 55 per cent of the amount over the lifetime allowance is levied by the taxman. In practice, it is hard to imagine how this particular rule will affect you.

TOP TIP

This doesn't affect you right now, but gives an idea of how useful tax relief can be for people who plan their finances carefully. Or you can pass on the idea to your mum or dad – in return for a few quid, or even some brownie points.

Say you are coming up to retirement and your company suggests you go early, 'sweetened' by a £40,000 lump sum redundancy payment, of which £30,000 is tax free.

You pop the £10,000 amount above that into a personal pension. The tax relief at 20 per cent means your pension fund has received an immediate uplift, worth an extra £2,500. Meanwhile, if you are a higher-rate taxpayer you claim back another £2,500 against your final tax bill.

You then retire and take 25 per cent of that pension investment as a tax-free lump sum – but thanks to the taxman's generosity, the extra lump sum you will receive is £3,125.

Who are personal pensions suitable for?

■ Anyone who is self-employed;

■ Employees where no company scheme is available; where some of the benefits are not applicable to their personal circumstances (what use is a dependants' pension if you are unmarried and without children?); or where the main scheme's investment strategy is massively out of kilter with your own (either on ethical or performance grounds).

HOW MUCH SHOULD YOU SAVE?

Hopefully, if you have got this far you finally accept the argument in favour of setting aside money for your retirement. The question you may now want an answer to is: how much should you actually save?

Ultimately, it all depends on how much you can afford. But the figures are uncompromising – and you should prepare for a shock.

The *Guardian* has a nifty online calculator that can help you work out how much to save, based on how much of a pension your monthly contributions will buy you.

Say you are a 25-year-old who wants to retire at 65 on a quarter of your current salary of £25,000 and expect to live for 20 years thereafter. This means you only want £6,250 a year, hardly a generous amount.

Coupled with a maximum state pension, it would mean a combined income of just under £11,000 a year, barely enough to survive on.

To achieve even this amount, you would need to start saving £100 a month for the next 40 years, increasing contributions by 3 per cent a month until retirement. The value of the funds would also have to grow by 3 per cent a year in real terms after inflation.

Retiring with the same pension at age 60, just five years earlier, would require the same person to save £155 a month.

What if you only start saving at 35? The Guardian calculator offers grim news: to retire at 65 on the same pension as before you need to save £166 a month. This rises to £296 a month for someone who is 45.

What is important to note here is that if you were to live longer than 20 years after retirement – and require a payout to last longer – you would have to save even more.

All this points to another useful fact: starting to save earlier will ultimately make life far easier for you, mainly because compound interest offers you far more years in which your funds will grow.

Contacts and links

The Pensions Advisory Service: www.pensionsadvisoryservice.org.uk

The Pensions Regulator: www.thepensionsregulator.gov.uk

12 Money and ethics

For the majority of us, ethics and finance tend to be placed in two separate compartments. We might live out our lives on the basis of a set of moral principles – religious, political, whatever they may be – but financial issues rarely enter into that equation. Yet increasing numbers of people are choosing to put their money where their consciences are.

Almost unnoticed by the big battalions of the financial services industry until recently, a new approach to investments is gaining ground in the UK. It is called ethical investment.

This, loosely described, is an approach which starts from the premise that the way we save our money can have both positive and negative consequences for the world in which we live.

It also accepts that we want our money to work for us in exactly the same way we lead our everyday lives, based on similar moral positions and promoting similar values.

Ethical finances work

Your individual actions won't change anything by themselves. But money does make the world go round, as they say.

In the last quarter of 2008, even after the stock market collapsed in the wake of the credit crunch, the UK's investment industry managed more than £5bn of ethical funds. Many tens of billions of pounds on top of that are being spent more 'ethically' because people show that they care about decisions made in their names.

Used collectively and correctly, all that money can make a tremendous difference for billions of other people across the world.

Equally importantly, it could also mean there is no longer a divide between our view of the world and how our money is used.

Is it possible to make ethical financial choices?

Yes. Almost every financial product allows you to choose an ethical alternative of some description, either in terms of the product itself or the company offering it.

You can also choose products that more closely reflect your specific ethical concerns.

For example:

- it is possible to decide whether your investments should promote environmental issues or avoid arms manufacture, tobacco sales or animal experiments. You can also promote 'positive engagement', rewarding companies that do good things;
- you can choose bank accounts with institutions that operate ethically;
- you can buy 'green' electricity from companies that will use some of your money to promote environmental concerns and reduce greenhouse gases;
- you can buy cars that pollute less;
- you can even choose to be buried in a more ethical way, using renewable sources for your coffin.

Ethical banking

Some banks are implicated in a range of unsavoury lending and business practices, not just in the UK but other parts of the world. As a result, it is easy to see why some people believe them to be unethical, not just in terms of their global policies, but also the way they treat their own customers here in this country.

Ironically, many UK banks are bowing to growing pressure to operate on the basis of a more ethical approach to their business practices. Many now make large play of their commitment to environmental and socially responsible investment, as well as charitable donations and sponsorship. If you are unconvinced by some or all of these claims, you have a number of options.

- **Building societies** originated in the self-help movement of 18th-century Britain. Many have grown into massive financial institutions. They are run by people who are unelected – annual meetings are, frankly, a charade. They can repossess a property and put someone on the street, or treat their staff shabbily.

  But they remain fully mutual, in other words owned by their members, and retain a little of the ethos of 19th-century mutuality. They don't indulge in the same excesses as the big banks and often give customers a better deal. They also offer almost identical mortgages, savings and current accounts as the banks.

- Look to the **Co-operative Bank** or its Internet offshoot **Smile** for your bank account. **Triodos Bank**, the UK offshoot of a Netherlands bank, also offers ethical deposit accounts. **Unity Trust Bank**, an offshoot of the trade union movement, also offers savings accounts, including a 14-day access account and a high-interest account. The **Ecology Building Society** is well known for its mortgages to help fund sustainable and ecologically sound homes. It also offers a wide range of savings schemes.

- **Credit unions** are among the biggest single sources of 'ethical' savings schemes in the UK. Essentially, they are democratically run financial co-operatives, in which all profits are shared. Credit unions are formed on the basis of workplace or geographical affiliations and at the last count there were more than 550 of them in the UK, with some 600,000 members. The Association of British Credit Unions is the place to go to for details.

- You may also want to look at Ethical Consumer magazine's online research tool, **Ethiscore**, which has listed the Internet banking arms of a number of banks and given them scores out of 20, based on a range of ethical criteria.

Ethical credit cards

The starting point – and a key challenge – for anyone who wants to have an 'ethical' credit card is that there is almost no choice other than to use one of two credit card companies, Visa and MasterCard.

Individual issuers use either Visa or MasterCard for their transactions, so ultimately you are giving them money every time you use your card. That said, both organisations claim they have firm ethical values. For example, MasterCard claims it is 'known globally for having among the highest standards of professional integrity and ethics in the business community'.

Visa's mission statement is very similar. In addition, the company says it is committed to financial literacy programmes to help people spend more wisely. It helps more than 20 such programmes in countries including Mexico, Indonesia, Brazil and China.

Assuming you believe either of those two companies' claims, can you make an ethical choice in terms of issuers? One option is to use an 'affinity card'. These work like normal credit cards, usually bearing the company's typical APR and featuring the usual cashback or introductory offers. However, they have the additional feature of being associated with organisations such as charities, businesses, sports teams or political parties. Your credit card company donates money to your chosen organisation according to how much you use your card. It will usually donate a set amount when you sign up for the affinity card (usually around £5), and then a nominal amount or percentage for every transaction you make.

Affinity cards are available from scores of organisations, including trades unions, ActionAid and Save the Children. The simplest way to find out if your organisation offers an affinity card is to go to its website and check. If it does not, think of a similar organisation operating in the same sector. It is likely that you will be able to find a card that suits your needs. Another option is the American Express RED card, backed by U2 singer Bono, which offers to donate 1 per cent of all purchases towards fighting Aids in Africa.

TOP TIP

Some affinity cards charge quite a high APR for people who don't pay off their debts in full each month.

If you are among the two thirds who do, an affinity card is a good idea, as your chosen charity receives a donation every time you use the card while you are paying no interest whatsoever. But if you pay off your debts more slowly, go for a card with a lower APR, or even a 0 per cent interest rate. You can then donate to the charity of your choice out of the savings you make from the lower interest you are paying on the card.

How 'going green' can save you money

It can be significantly cheaper to go green. In other words, you can make your contribution towards saving the planet and pay less. Here are some ideas on how to go about it.

Motoring. Switch to a smaller-engine car, or one that has less harmful emissions. You will both cut running costs and pay less road tax. Use alternative transport when you can; trains, buses and bicycles are less polluting and/or cheaper (although in the case of trains you have to book ahead to see any real price benefits).

Your home. A staggering £1 in every £3 spent on heating is currently being wasted through the 10.3 million homes in the UK with insufficient insulation. Many homes are also overheated, with thermostats set at too-high levels. You could save two tonnes of CO_2 a year – and up to £500 – by making your home energy efficient:

- make sure your loft is properly insulated and consider cavity insulation;
- fit double or secondary glazing;

- check that your central heating boiler is as energy-efficient as possible. If it was fitted more than 10 years ago, it probably no longer is;
- turn down your heating by one degree centigrade and reduce by 30 minutes a day the period it is on;
- switch off all lights if you are not in the room, plus your computer when you are not working/browsing;
- fit energy-saving light bulbs;
- if you have a wooden floor, insulate between joists;
- fit draft excluders to your front door, windows and any room that you use regularly;
- if replacing electrical appliances such as washing machines, dishwashers and fridges, look for those that save energy. Always use the lowest-possible heat and water settings and make sure you fully load each machine to cut down the times it is used;
- if money is slightly less of an issue, you may also want to consider switching energy supplies to a 'green' utilities supplier.

Food. Confine major spending to once a month and buy in bulk. Have the items delivered by the store: you save massively in time, as well as petrol costs. For smaller day-to-day items, walk or cycle to your local shop, or catch a bus.

If you have a garden, you may also want to consider growing your own vegetables. Those who do say it is remarkably easy, produces amazing food and can be incredibly therapeutic.

Clothes. Cheap foreign imports are very tempting. But while it may make sense to buy lots of cheap clothes, you may want to restrict yourself to fewer items, thereby saving on global shipping costs – as well as money in your own wallet.

Ethical investment

Ethical investment is the general term given to the process whereby money is invested on the basis of a set of moral principles.

These principles can be fairly wide and, as a result, so is the scope for people to make decisions about the ones they hold to be most important.

The fundamental aim of ethical investment is to ensure that your money makes a difference – either by persuading companies not to do things that are 'unethical' (by not buying their shares), or by rewarding them for being ethical (and encouraging others to do the same) by investing in them.

Screening

The way in which investment takes place is on the basis of 'screening'. This can be either 'negative', 'positive' or both.

In other words, a fund manager whom you entrust with your money is required to draw up a set of issues that are regarded as so important that they will determine whether he or she can buy shares in a company being screened.

Examples of negative screening, where certain shares will be excluded, are firms engaged in the manufacture or sale of arms, alcohol, tobacco, gambling, animal testing and environmental damage or which pay exploitative wages in developing countries.

Positive screening could include waste management businesses, environmental technology, public transport, education, telecommunications and renewable energy.

Firms that offer good working conditions, energy-efficient buildings and corporate recycling policies might also be considered in a broadly positive light.

The aim of the fund manager is to look at the shares available to invest in and create a viable portfolio that offers the opportunity of capital growth, income, or both.

Ethical financial advice

As the market for ethical finance products has grown, more and more financial advisers are willing and able to offer guidance on some of the key investment decisions that clients may wish to take.

For that, you probably need someone who is more of a 'holistic' financial planner, with long-standing experience of more than a few stock ethical funds that he or she can place a client into. Someone, for example, who can distinguish between deeply held environmental concerns, those of a vegan or those of an active trade unionist.

The Ethical Investment Association (EIA) brings together financial advisers from around the UK who are dedicated to the promotion of ethical and socially responsible investment (SRI). Its members are committed to increasing access to advice in all areas of ethical and socially responsible investment, and to increasing and improving their own professional knowledge.

Contacts and links

Ethical Investment Research Service: www.eiris.org

Green Electricity Marketplace: www.greenelectricity.org

Ethical Investment Association: www.ethicalinvestment.org.uk

UK Social Investment Forum: www.uksif.org

PART IV Budgeting

13
Money and your budget

For anyone who has made use of one or more of sections in this book, or even just flicked through it, the one thing that ought to stand out is the need to get the best value out of any financial transaction we engage in.

This all forms part of a central concept: using your money carefully, budgeting to spend what you can afford, never paying more than you need to for anything and always getting the best for your money.

If you already do all these things, you may be part of an unusual breed of person who manages to balance his or her budget effectively and does not need any additional help to look after your money. But if we are honest, none of us is perfect when it comes to managing our finances. We make mistakes, occasionally find ourselves in trouble and need help to dig ourselves out of it.

This section of the book is designed to help you do that. It contains a number of concepts linked to budgeting:

- how to prepare a budget
- how to spend less but still get the same lifestyle
- where to cut costs in a hurry
- where to get help with debts

Preparing a budget

In theory, this ought to be a fairly simple process.

You start by looking at your bank statement. This ought to tell you two crucial things, at least one of which you should know perfectly well: how much you earn every month – although if you don't even know that, you are probably in a bit more trouble than we thought!

Once you know how much you earn, it should not be difficult to work out how much you are spending, certainly in the big areas.

There are, nowadays, many different online calculators that can help you do that. But it is easy enough to do it on paper. Here are the main expenses you should be able to work out:

- rent/mortgage
- council tax
- commuting
- gas
- electricity
- water
- telephone bills (including mobiles)
- food
- TV licence

These are, essentially, all 'necessary' items you need to spend money on every month. Almost all, apart from food, will be fairly regular and predictable amounts, many of which will probably be paid by standing order or direct debit. That said, there are ways of economising on each of these items.

The next element of spending is still 'necessary' but consists of unexpected items that we are likely to face from time to time. Again, it is likely that most of these will be itemised in some form in your bank statement. If they are one-off bills, add them up over a year and divide by 12: the chances are you will need to create a small emergency pot of money to take care of these items as and when they crop up.

- car and household repairs and maintenance
- dentist and optician bills
- insurance (car, home contents etc)

The final part involves less necessary items. That's not to say they don't feel necessary: indeed, life could seem quite bleak without one or two of them. But these are items which you could probably do without for a while, at a pinch.

- going out/entertainment (drinks, films, clubs, restaurant meals); don't forget the bottle of wine you take to someone else's party
- smoking
- newspapers or magazines
- coffees to and from work
- canteen at work, or bought sandwiches

- sweets/chocolates/crisps and other 'treats' such as hairdressers etc
- unnecessary food and clothes
- holidays, weekends away

This ought to be easy. In practice, many of us are binge shoppers: there are some weeks when we spend little, other weeks when we splurge out. The chances are four weeks should provide you with a good average. Don't forget to add in the little things, like the loaf of bread and pint of milk from the corner shop.

Because many of the items are one-off, paid for in cash and therefore not so obvious in any monthly statement, it may be difficult to work out how much you spend on each. If it really is impossible, one way is to keep a record going forward of what you are spending every day. Keep this up for a couple of weeks and you'll have a good idea of how much you are spending.

Another way is to keep all your receipts for a month in an envelope, then add them up.

How to cut your spending

Once you know what you are spending every month, you can then move on to the next phase of the budget process: cutting your expenses. There are essentially two main ways.

1 The first is to maintain the same lifestyle but look for cheaper ways to do it. That means seeking out better deals on just about everything,

including insurance, energy bills and so on. Shopping around, in other words. Check out www.moneysavingexpert.com for tips.

Make sure you are getting the best deal on your fuel and that you are on the best tariff. Often you can get further concessions if you obtain your gas and electricity from the same supplier – a facility known as 'dual fuel' deals.

You can get further discounts by paying by direct debit and opting for paperless billing.

Consider switching to metered water if your consumption is low – quite likely if you live alone or are there are just two of you in the house.

Check out bundled packages for television, broadband and telephone, to see if you can save money by switching. While you are at it, consider if you really need one of the more expensive packages anyway.

2 The second is actively to cut things out of your spending and making do without. This is more difficult. One of the simplest ways is to set yourself a budget of, say, £60 for weekly food shopping, or £100 a month for clothes.

Write down a list of priorities that need money spending on each week and month – and stick to it religiously.

Every penny counts: walk past the ready meals in the supermarket and pick up some pasta and fresh vegetables instead – cheaper and better for you. You may be surprised that supermarket own brands often taste just as good and sometimes better than premium branded goods.

It may sound like an old housewife's trick, but some people find it easiest to create separate 'jars' or 'envelopes' into which they stick money every month or even every week. Each jar/envelope is clearly labelled and if you take more money out of one, you have to make up for it by economising from another jar.

Does this sound a bit too childish? Do you feel it is too ridiculous to work? There are actually a wide variety of websites that use this approach, with many thousands of people who use virtual 'jars' or 'envelopes' to manage their money successfully.

Almost certainly, the first few weeks after you set yourself a new and restricted budget will be hellishly difficult. You will wonder how to manage. But everyone who tries this system finds that over a period of two or three months it becomes second nature.

TOP TIP

Many people find that spending certain amounts over time becomes automatic. This applies just as much to over-spending as it does to keeping your belt tightened. Once you have managed to keep within a new budget for two or three months, the entire process should become automatic, too, and you won't even notice the fact that you are spending less.

Dealing with bad debts

We've already talked about how to deal with debts you have had to incur as a student. For some people though, debt becomes a habit and the situation starts to spin out of control. They may owe many thousands of pounds to a wide variety of creditors. In this case, it's too late simply to plan a budget and hope that any problems can be resolved by reigning in spending.

What often happens here is that people can sense what is happening. They know that they are sinking deeper and deeper into trouble. At the same time, they are getting more and more depressed by what is happening: creditors are probably chasing them for money all the time.

Some will lapse into apathy, chucking bank statements or bills unopened into a kitchen drawer – 'brown envelope syndrome'. The only psychological relief they get, ironically, is by spending even more money, 'treating' themselves to expensive and unnecessary items to overcome what is now a serious and growing problem. And even at this point, some people cannot even admit to what is happening to them.

If any of this is starting to sound like you, you really need a different – and much tougher – approach to dig yourself out of the hole you are in. Here are the steps you need to follow.

- Admit the problem. There is no point in hoping it will go away – it won't. Throwing away your bank statements without opening them and ignoring letters from companies you owe money to will only get you further into trouble.

- Work out how much you owe. This is not usually too difficult: add up what is in all the stroppy letters and final demands you have received in the past few months and you should have a pretty good idea. By the way, don't ignore those debts where the creditor appears to have gone silent: he or she almost certainly hasn't and is probably talking to the bailiffs right now.

- Stop saving money. Bizarre as it may seem, some people can be in debt while still tucking small sums of money away every month. Yet the interest you get on any savings will almost certainly be lower than the rate of interest you are paying out on loans, mortgages and credit cards. Worse, if you are working, savings interest will be taxed. The best way to get your savings to work for you is by using them to pay off your debts.

- Reclaim money owed to you. This could be anything from debts owed to you by family or friends, to tax overpayments and unfair bank charges. If you have become unemployed – not uncommon in the current climate – make sure you are claiming all the benefits and allowances due to you. Many people don't bother, assuming they will soon be back at work and don't need to. Don't fall for that: every penny counts. Claim fare and entrance concessions and free prescriptions if you are entitled to them.

- Calculate how much can afford to pay back towards your debts. A useful rule of thumb is a maximum of 50 per cent of monthly net income – and that includes any credit you have taken out: credit cards, loans, a mortgage, overdraft, hire purchase deals on a car and so on. In addition, no more than 20 per cent of take-home income should go on other standing bills, such as utilities (water, electricity, gas, telephone), TV licence payments and so on. This may not seem like much, but the rest of your income needs to go on other regular household bills, plus food, travel and so on.

- Decide what types of debt are most important. The most essential task is to protect the roof over your head. If you lose that, you are in big trouble. So prioritise your rent or mortgage payments.

- Prioritise any other bills where you risk going to jail or being fined in court if you don't pay up. This includes council and other taxes, including income tax or your TV licence. Non-payment of council tax means the money may be taken from your wages or benefits. If that does not work, bailiffs may be called in. Imprisonment is an option, so try to avoid it. Fuel debts – because you face disconnection for non-payment – and hire purchase on essential items should also be given top priority.

- If you have problems with repaying your mortgage you should make an appointment to talk to your lender at the earliest opportunity. Don't miss payments. Handing over the keys to your home to the mortgage company or declaring yourself bankrupt may seem a quick fix to overwhelming debt, but both can have long-term repercussions.

- Prepare to negotiate with your creditors. Once you have decided what are 'primary' and 'secondary' debts, it's time to talk. You should find most creditors will be anxious to strike a deal. At the end of the day, they know that if they don't, they risk the possibility of you not paying their bills at all.

- If you need help, talk to experts at the Citizens Advice office In your area, as they are experienced and have helped thousands of people like you. The Consumer Credit Counselling Service (CCCS) charity will also help. By the way: NEVER pay for debt counselling, or any firms that claim to be able to help sort out your debts. They are charging you for free advice – and they may not be able to help anyway.

- Don't ever think a deal with creditors will be plain sailing thereafter: you will be expected to make certain sacrifices in order to pay back the money you owe. If you agree a repayment schedule, stick to it. There's nothing guaranteed to make creditors go mad than someone who goes back on a deal.

TOP TIP

*Ignore pressure and threats from some creditors. You may receive letters, phone calls, even doorstep visits telling you that you should pay one creditor rather than another. Look at every single communication from creditors through the prism of what is, ultimately, a primary payment that **must** be made, or a secondary one that can wait a bit or receive a smaller repayment. At the end of the day,* *every penny that you give one creditor means less for another, perhaps more important, one.*

Debt consolidation

Wouldn't it be so much easier to amalgamate what you owe, get a deal which costs you less every month and simply pay it all off to a single source?

Every year, hundreds of thousands of people have the same idea. Research by the Office of Fair Trading (OFT), the consumer debt watchdog, found that tens of billions of pounds of secured and unsecured lending is used for debt consolidation every year.

In addition, researchers Mori Financial Services have found that about 15 per cent of last credit card balance transfers – where you get a 0 per cent credit card deal – involves consolidation of more than one credit card balance into a single card.

The potential advantages of debt consolidation can be:

- lower interest rates
- lower monthly payments
- having to deal with only one creditor.

However, there are disadvantages too, and many people don't realise that there can be costs involved:

- the costs of settling an existing loan, such as redemption penalties, and arranging a new one (possibly including broker commission) can be significant;

■ as we saw in Chapter 7, many loan providers tend to 'piggyback' payment protection insurance (PPI) on their loans, sometimes without borrowers understanding what they are paying for.

The OFT's research found that most borrowers do not shop around for credit for debt consolidation, although this can save money – two thirds of borrowers who consolidated debts obtained information from only one provider before going ahead.

Moreover, many borrowers, particularly those in financial distress, are unaware of other alternatives which are open to them, such as negotiating with creditors themselves or getting help from free debt counselling services.

Contacts and links

Price comparison websites

Nowadays it is possible to get a much better deal on a range of financial products by shopping online. Here are some financial comparison websites that can tell you which products are best for you.

Moneyfacts: www. moneyfacts.co.uk

Moneysupermarket: www.moneysupermarket.com

uSwitch: www.uswitch.co.uk

Moneyextra: www.moneyextra.com

Confused.com: www.confused.com

GoCompare: www.gocompare.com

MoneyExpert: www.moneyexpert.com

Protecting your money

This section is about insurance. Putting it bluntly like this is, without a shadow of doubt, almost guaranteed to make you want either to turn the page or put the book down altogether.

Insurance is, after all, a deadly boring topic and no sane person would want to read about it unless they are forced to, would they?

That's possibly true, but let me try to persuade you to persevere.

The fact is that none of us can do without insurance in one or more of its forms. In some cases, it is a legal requirement: if you don't have cover for your car, you are not allowed to drive on the main road. In other cases, you will end up having your arm twisted to take out insurance: any mortgage lender will think twice about offering a loan if you don't have protection in the event of something happening to your home.

At some point in your life, perhaps bizarrely, having insurance can even be seen as an act of love: if you are in a relationship or have children, you may want to protect them in case anything happens to you.

In every case, knowing what kind of cover you need and why, getting it at the best price and avoiding some of the expensive pitfalls involved in buying insurance are essential.

So what are the main kinds of cover you may need to consider?

- car insurance
- home and contents insurance
- travel insurance
- life insurance
- income protection
- payment protection

Car insurance

Of all the financial products sold in the UK, there is no doubt that car insurance is the one most commonly held by consumers.

This is hardly surprising: alone among so-called 'personal lines' cover – policies that protect your life, home, health or income – car insurance is the only one that it is compulsory to have. If you are stopped while driving without it, prepare to be prosecuted.

In theory, this ought to make everyone a car insurance expert. After all, here is a classic 'grudge' purchase, one we resent paying too much for. What better reason could there be for knowing every trick in the book that helps bring the cost of premiums down?

The irony is that, by and large, most of us tend to stick with the same insurer for too long. We only change policies when premiums become noticeably too dear. And few of us bother looking through the small print on our policies – with all sorts of dire consequences when it comes to making a claim.

Don't play the fronting game

By the way, one of the common misconceptions among people in their teens and 20s is that they can ignore the subject of car cover because their parents will simply add their car to the family policy, with them as a 'named driver'.

If that's what you think, prepare to be disappointed: insurance companies call this 'fronting' and will usually disqualify a claim if they believe the car is owned by the named driver and not by the insured party. In some cases, especially if accidents are involved, the police may prosecute young drivers without proper insurance.

All details such as who bought the car, in whose name the vehicle registration document is, who pays for the road tax, where the car is kept most of the time are all things that will be considered by the insurer when considering whether to pay out on a claim.

Besides, the longer you are named on your parents' policy, the less of a no-claims bonus you will have: at some stage it makes sense to cut the apron strings.

What types of motor policies are there?

The minimum type of motor insurance you can take out is 'third party'. This covers liability for:

■ injuries to other people, including passengers
■ damage to other people's property
■ passengers for accidents caused by them
■ damage arising from the use of caravan or trailer while attached to the car

185

The next step up is 'third party, fire and theft'. This provides the above cover, plus fire or theft of the vehicle.

'Comprehensive' insurance provides cover for the above, plus:

- accidental damage to your car
- personal accident benefit
- medical expenses
- loss of or damage to personal effects in the car

And by the way, if you're wondering why car insurance is so expensive it's largely because other drivers have failed to bite the bullet and buy insurance. Official statistics say that one in 20 drivers is uninsured, but recent research carried out by Direct Line and Mori suggests that this figure is more like one in 10 drivers. This adds around £30 to the average annual premium.

What about my quote?

There are various other factors that affect how expensive your own quote might be. These include:

- **Postcode.** You are deemed to be higher risk if you live in a city or urban area, especially if you park your car in the street. Security measures – alarms, locks and so on – reduce premiums.
- **Age and experience.** Newly qualified drivers – or drivers under 25 – are deemed more likely to have accidents than older, more experienced drivers.

This has important lessons for parents: adding teenage drivers to a policy can significantly increase their premiums. It is sometimes cheaper to add a teenager on a temporary basis, for example during a holiday.

Attending special courses, such as the PassPlus (www.passplus.org.uk) scheme, aimed at new drivers and designed by the Driving Standards Agency, also helps. This is a certificate where a young driver who has already passed his or her driving test receives specific lessons in night, motorway and town traffic driving. Achieving the PassPlus can earn significant discounts (as much as 35 per cent) on your car insurance.

- **Claims history.** The less you claim, the less you pay. Five-year no-claims discounts are best.
- **Excess.** The more money you're willing to pay out as excess, the lower your premium. The average excess is £200, but can be higher.

Buying insurance: the information you need

Make sure you have the following information to hand:

- car make and model
- registration number
- full post code
- number of years of no claims discount
- where the car is normally kept – street, garage etc
- what the car will be used for – social, domestic and pleasure; or business
- estimated annual mileage
- type of cover – comprehensive, third party fire and theft, or third party only
- full details of claims or convictions in the last three years. Don't lie. If you get caught out, your claim will be barred

How to cut the cost of your car insurance

The obvious point is that you should shop around at least once a year – every time you renew your insurance. But it is also the case that people pay for the level of cover they have. The more bolt-on 'goodies', the higher the cost of their insurance.

So decide which of the following you want and which you don't need.

- Is a courtesy car provided as standard? Is it offered if your car is stolen or written-off? Do you have to pay extra to insure the courtesy car?

- Is motor legal protection included?

- Does the policy offer roadside breakdown assistance?

- Do you pay extra for overseas cover?

- How high is the policy excess? Are there any mandatory excesses for accidental or malicious damage?

- Does cover include personal injury, personal belongings or replacement locks?

- Does it offer legal advice and medical counselling telephone lines?

- Will your insurer immediately authorise repairs from recommended agents?

- Will your no-claims bonus be affected if the accident wasn't your fault or the cost cannot be recovered?

- Can you transfer a no-claims bonus built up while driving on somebody else's insurance?

- Can you transfer your no-claims bonus on to a second car?

- Can you protect your no-claims bonus? How many claims are you allowed under the scheme before your no-claims bonus is affected?

- When you make a claim, do you speak to the broker who sold you the policy or the insurer?

- Will you be charged extra for paying by monthly direct debit?

TOP TIP

What else can you do to get cheap young driver car insurance? Sad as it may sound, forget about turbo-charged cars with big spoilers, fat tyres, alloy rims and other 'sexy' extras. For at least two years after passing your test, aim to drive a car that has a small engine, or is in the lowest possible insurance group.

Home and contents insurance

For many young people in their 20s, home insurance is a luxury they feel they can do without.

After all, most will be renting a property and, quite rightly, the cost of upkeep of the fabric of the building is up to the landlord. But contents cover is another matter: if all your belongings were stolen or destroyed, how would you replace them? One thing is certain: your landlord won't pay for them and neither will his or her insurance.

Regardless of who pays, too many people pay too much for their cover. Or else they discover, usually too late, that the protection they thought they had was not up to the job. So how should you approach taking out either type of cover?

One of the most important points to realise is that shopping around can save hundreds of pounds a year in premiums. Here are some other issues to look at when taking out either policy.

Premiums

These are based on an interlocking combination of factors:

- the value of a home or its contents. Typically, this is defined less as the purchase price of the home itself, or even its current value, but how much it would cost to rebuild, theoretically taking account of specific factors such as obtaining access to a site, the materials involved and so on;

- its postcode. People living in inner-city areas often pay more because insurers believe there is a higher risk of burglary and/or vandalism;

- the type of property. As above, homes of unusual construction – such as thatched cottages – are more expensive to insure, partly because of the added risks involved;

- individual claims history. This is pretty obvious: the more you claim, the more you pay.

Levels of cover

Assuming that all policies are equal is a potentially dangerous mistake.

A basic policy will cover you for a series of specified risks. These include storms, fire, lightning, explosion, subsidence, thieves and vandals.

But it is often sensible to make sure that the policy also covers frost damage to pipes and accidental damage to underground pipes and cables.

Moreover, damage to a home – and its contents – often happens not so much because of a cataclysmic event but by accident, frequently caused by the occupier. Cover against such damage, for example a ruined carpet or accidents to wallpaper and furniture, is usually a sound move.

By the way, remember that in the event of a fire, for example, you will be suffering damage that may need to be claimed from both home and contents insurance at the same time. Your landlord's kitchen units, for instance, should be covered as a 'fixed item' under his or her home policy, because they are generally anchored to a wall. But a freestanding cupboard might not be.

A good policy should also cover your legal liability, as the owner, in the event of an injury to a visitor that leads to you being sued.

Exclusions

Most policies have standard exclusions, things for which you are not covered. They include:

- damage caused because your house has not been kept in a good state of repair;
- costs of routine wear and tear;
- deliberate damage by the insured party (you, that is);
- smoke damage;
- damage caused by pets;
- belongings outside the home, such as laptop computers, cameras or jewellery, although this can be remedied by taking out an 'all-risks' policy.

Most house contents policies put limits on the amount that can be claimed for specified valuable items, such as electrical goods, jewellery and works of art.

There is often a single-item limit of £1,000 or so and an overall limit of £10,000 for all your valuables. If you have items of greater value, make sure that you check first with an insurer, or a broker, to see if you are covered.

Theft and damage are not usually covered if you are away from your home for a long period – usually 30 consecutive days.

Choosing a policy

When taking out a contents policy, you have two main types to choose from.

- New-for-old – this does what it says on the tin. If your belongings are stolen or damaged beyond repair, the policy will pay for the cost of a brand new replacement. Note that this does not mean you will automatically be given the money to buy what you want. More and more insurers replace items themselves; partly as an anti-fraud measure but also because they get discounts on bulk purchases.
- Indemnity cover – gives you the current value of your items, often a fraction of the replacement cost. Such policies are often cheaper, but potentially risky in the event of a major burglary or serious damage, such as a fire. Note, too, that underclothing and linen are covered only on an indemnity basis, even under most new-for-old policies: if your wardrobe consists mainly of Armani, Prada and Christian Dior, look for policies that pay the full replacement value.

How much cover

The sums you insure for are generally based on two approaches: 'bedroom-rated' or 'sum insured'.

A bedroom-rated policy. Your premiums are based on the number of bedrooms in your house. Generally, though not always, the valuation is generous enough to ensure that you are amply covered. However, such policies are sometimes slightly more expensive.

A sum-insured policy. You have to calculate the value of your contents yourself. The advantage is that you set down exactly how much all your possessions are worth and their replacement cost. The disadvantage is that the process is, initially, more time-consuming. Also, you risk under-insuring: any claims may then be scaled down by the proportion by which you are unprotected. For example, say your contents are worth £20,000, but you took out cover for £10,000. A fire then causes £10,000, or 50% of damage to your possessions. When you claim, any payment will be made at 50% of the amount you insured for: £5,000.

How to cut the cost of cover

- Generally, you pay the first £50 or £100 of every claim yourself. This is a 'compulsory excess'. You may also have the choice of higher excesses, in return for which the insurer will reduce premiums.
- Don't claim. No-claims discounts are becoming increasingly common.
- Ask about 'loyalty discounts' for staying with an insurer for a long time. But don't ignore that fact that shopping around may be cheaper.
- Don't ignore insurance brokers. The Internet is often very cheap, but many brokers can offer policies that are just as competitive, as well as more closely matching your specific needs. Moreover, with brokers you can often get them to cut the cost of their quote by telling them that you have obtained a cheaper one elsewhere – they simply sacrifice some of their sales commission. Don't try to lie, however: they know the 'real' cost of cover and they will simply send you on your way.

TOP TIP

If you are sharing rented property, ALWAYS tell your contents insurer. Premiums are sometimes more expensive, to compensate for the fact that some insurers believe there are greater risks involved in providing cover. Or check your policy carefully, as the small print in some may invalidate a claim for people who share.

Travel insurance

Travel insurance. Isn't that something you simply get from an agent at the time of booking a foreign trip? Or a last-minute optional extra to be picked up at the airport, along with magazines for the flight and a blockbuster novel?

It is not too difficult to understand why travel cover can generate such feelings of *boredom*. The wonderful thing about a holiday is that it should liberate you from the drudgery of everyday life, of which any type of insurance is most definitely a part.

And in any event, is it really necessary, particularly for holidays within Europe?

Do you need travel insurance?

Most of us, thankfully, take it for granted that if we step outside Europe we will want protection of some sort: there are too many stories of huge hospital bills or of being sued for millions by victims of a car accident, for people to ignore taking out travel insurance.

As for Europe, you are entitled to reciprocal state-provided health services within the European Economic Area (EU countries, plus Iceland, Liechtenstein and Norway).

For this you need a form called European Health Insurance Card (EHIC), available through all post offices, albeit with a 21-day wait. You can also call a special hotline: 0845 606 2030 – and wait 10 days for one.

You can also apply for it FREE from the NHS website: www.nhs.uk (ignore the many other websites that offer to help you apply for it – in return for a £9.95 fee).

However, the level of treatment you receive is based on what the state provides for its own citizens, which may not always be what you could expect here in the UK.

More importantly, an EHIC will not deliver immediate repatriation in the event of serious injury. Yet the cost of an air ambulance from Spain to the UK alone can be as much as £9,000.

In any event, travel insurance is not only about health. It also covers problems such as liability to third parties, theft, loss of personal possessions, flight cancellation and so on.

On balance, then, we have to conclude that in nearly all cases the answer is: you need to be insured.

Travel operators' products or your own cover?

Up to 80 per cent of people take out insurance offered by travel agents when they book their holiday.

Yet research suggests that travel insurance costs up to twice as much when booked through an operator instead of being bought separately. You also pay 17.5 per cent insurance premium tax, instead of

5 per cent if cover is taken out via an intermediary, or directly from the insurer.

Annual or single travel policy

The explosion of cheap airfares means far more people travel abroad than ever before. Despite this fact, the Foreign Office found recently that while 13 per cent of UK residents fail to take out adequate insurance in relation to all travel abroad, this rises to 43 per cent of travellers who go on short breaks.

If you are likely to be travelling abroad more than once a year, including short breaks, it makes sense to take out annual cover.

Why? One simple reason: it is much cheaper than taking out cover every time you are about to take off.

Things to watch out for

- Pre-existing medical conditions: if you have one, you must inform your insurer before taking out the policy or you may not be covered. When looking for cover, a simple tip is to contact the support organisation related to your medical condition: they will know who can offer insurance.

- Period of trip: most annual travel insurance policies are for up to 31 days at a time, so if you are planning to stay away for longer, you may need a specific policy that allows you to do that. There are several types of 'backpacker' policy available.

- Winter sports: increasing numbers of people want to ski for a couple of weeks. Not only is it important to have a certain amount of ski cover, but if you intend to take part in certain 'intensive' winter sports (off-piste skiing, for example), make sure that, too, is covered. Also, if you are a regular skier, specialist insurance may be necessary to protect against theft of skis from roof racks, lack of snow, ski lifts being closed and so on.

- 'Extreme sports': most policies don't cover microlighting, mountaineering or parachuting, so be sure to check.

- Travelling separately: if you and your partner make different overseas trips, you will want protection for this. Not all policies offer this, so ask.

- Possessions: insurers will often set limits on the amount that can be claimed for individual possessions stolen at the same time. This may mean that a £400 camera claim is reduced to a fraction of what it is worth. Check before you take out the cover.

TOP TIP

Travel insurance often duplicates cover you may already have available under the terms of home contents 'all-risks' policies. Some insurers offer discounts of up to 10–15 per cent for excluding certain items (camcorders, portable computers) from their travel cover. If in doubt, ask.

Life insurance

Talk to any financial adviser and the first thing he or she will tell you is that, before you do anything else with your money – invest it, start a personal pension with it, buy a house – the most important step is to protect what you already have. In other words, insure against things happening that may have a negative impact on your life.

But before you fall for the salesman's soft soap and buy any life cover, ask yourself one key question: do you need it? If you are a single person, not in a serious relationship, without kids or a mortgage to worry about, the chances are that you do not need any cover.

If you do need cover, it is worth bearing in mind that many employers already have a limited form of life insurance available through their companies. So always check with your human resources office first.

How much life cover?

OK, so you REALLY need cover. If so, how much? The simplest calculation, one adopted by many salespeople, is simply to multiply the income-earner's salary by 20.

This is because it is estimated that the lump sum available from the life insurance policy will deliver an income of about 5 per cent without too much risk of erosion of capital. Both partners in a relationship take out cover in relation to their own earnings.

A more sophisticated approach is to calculate current income and expenses, mortgage and other assets, plus whatever existing protection you have, adding and deleting various items before coming up with a sum that you need to protect yourself for.

What type of cover?

There are two main types of life cover.

Whole-of-life. This is a policy where, as long as premiums are kept up to date, a payout will be made upon your death, whenever that happens. Premiums are invested in the stock market, after taking out expenses and the provision of immediate cover.

But recent share price falls have meant that premiums are much higher at review times and often become prohibitive as people reach retirement age. As a result, most insurers no longer try to push this type of life cover on their unsuspecting punters.

Term cover. This is now much more common. Again, this is a simple policy to understand: you insure your life for a set number of years for an agreed amount. If you die, the policy pays out. If you don't die, the policy lapses at the end the term.

As mortality rates have improved in the past decade or so, the cost of term cover has fallen. This means that if you took out term assurance as little as five years ago, you should seek out a fresh quote: it may well be cheaper than what you are paying now.

Other points to note

Joint life

The chances are that if you are taking out cover, you are seeking to protect another person you care for, usually because you have taken out a joint mortgage.

If you ever have children, you might want to take out a separate policy each. But if not, a joint life policy is often cheaper.

This has some variants:

- 'first death' covers both your lives and pays out once on the death of the first of you to die;

199

■ 'last survivor' pays out once on the death of the second of you to die. For protecting dependants, the 'first death' option is usually the more appropriate.

Writing a policy in trust

When you take out life insurance, you don't want payouts to fall foul of inheritance tax. Moreover, you want the money to go to your partner quickly, without having to settle the estate first.

Writing an insurance policy in trust avoids these problems by ensuring that the policy pays out direct to your dependants, bypassing your estate altogether.

Most insurance companies have standard forms for doing this.

TOP TIP

If you take out a policy and the relationship breaks down, ask yourself whether you really need to pay into the scheme.

Income protection

All of us worry about different things. Oddly enough, the one thing we rarely think about is how we would survive financially if something awful happened but we carried on living – not just for a year or two but quite possibly indefinitely.

That's where permanent health insurance, or PHI, comes in. PHI pays out in the event of an illness that prevents you from working.

It will pay up to 60 per cent of your salary free of tax (or 75 per cent if it is an employer's policy – but you are taxed on the income) either until you are able to resume work again or until the plan expires, typically at 50, 55, 60 or 65 years of age.

Like other types of insurance, PHI contracts are agreed for a certain number of years, usually until retirement, or earlier by agreement.

Before you buy PHI

Check whether you have some form of PHI cover through your employer.

If you haven't, find out what your employer's sick payment scheme offers. This is because generally, though not always, PHI policies are timed to kick in after a sickness scheme runs out.

Now you have to decide on the following:

- when you want your PHI to start: this can be at any time from four weeks to two years after you become ill, depending on the plan. The longer you hold out, the lower the cost of monthly premiums;
- which type of cover you want. There are three types:
  1. level cover: benefits and contributions remain level through the plan term. This is cheapest, but the benefits will be eroded by inflation;
  2. increasing claim: benefits increase by 5 per cent during the course of a claim. Premiums will be extremely expensive at the outset;
  3. increasing cover: both benefits and contributions increase by 5 per cent annually. You are trying to match premiums with income, which is a bit cheaper in the long run;

- how much income you want to protect;
- whether you need 'waiver of premium'. This ensures that your premiums continue to be paid while you remain unable to work – yes, you need to keep paying premiums while drawing PHI;
- which to choose between 'own occupation' or 'any occupation'. The former means that the policy will pay out if you are unable to do your own job. The latter means it pays out if you cannot do ANY job. For example, the insurer might argue that a former steeplejack who is now in a wheelchair can still work in an office.

As before, the better the policy, the more you pay. If you take a lower-paid job after a period of illness, you may only be entitled to a portion of your PHI benefit, as the amount received would be based on the ratio of your drop in income to your original income.

Watch out for

- Medical evidence is always required. Cover may be more expensive for those in poor health and existing medical conditions may be excluded.
- Don't over-insure: if total income after a claim exceeds 60 per cent of pre-claim income, the policy will not pay out the full amount in the event of a claim.
- There may well be restrictions on working/travelling abroad.

How much does PHI cost?

A male aged 25, protecting an income of £20,000 a year until the age of 60, would pay upwards of £37 a month. A woman the same age would expect to pay £62 a month.

However unfair it might seem, premiums are almost always higher for a woman than for a man of the same age and occupation: statistics show that women are more likely on average to suffer ill health during working ages than men.

TOP TIP

Watch out for 'reviewable' policies. Companies will buy business with low premiums, only to increase them in later years. For example, if overall claims (not your individual ones, but those of all policyholders) are greater than anticipated, premiums can rise across the board. Not all policies are like this so check before you buy.

Payment protection

One of the things you'll rapidly discover when you take out a loan is that your potential lender will be extremely keen to sell you insurance to protect your payments in the event of something happening to you.

In fact, so keen are they that when you receive a quote for a loan over the phone, there's a strong chance that the monthly repayment figure you will be given includes an element for so-called payment protection insurance, or PPI.

PPI meets the loan payments on your behalf if you are unable to make them as a result of 'accident, sickness or unemployment'.

Payments can either be for a fixed period or, more often, they are indefinite: they end when your loan does.

Heavy sales tactics

Currently, up to 60 per cent of borrowers have some form of loan-related PPI cover, usually purchased from their lenders at the time they took out their loan.

This is a very high proportion, even higher than the equivalent mortgage protection product, which is strange, given that most loans are not 'secured'. This means that unlike mortgages, your home is not at risk if you are unable to pay off a loan.

The only serious explanation for such a high uptake is the high-pressure sales tactics that lenders use when giving out quotes, plus the perception of many borrowers that they won't get their money unless they sign up for PPI cover.

Why mortgage protection may be necessary

There is one type of payment protection cover that some people do find necessary, called Mortgage Payment Protection Insurance, or MPPI.

- There is no state help to meet the interest on a loan, never mind the capital repayments, if you are unable to work for any reason. The current recession means MPPI could come in handy if anything happens to your job.

But should YOU take out mortgage protection? Before you do, work out whether you really need it.

- You may well have some money saved up for a rainy day that could tide you over for a few months in the event of an emergency.

- If you fell ill, your employer might have a good sickness scheme in place. This could help you meet your loan repayments.

- If you are made redundant, you might have received a payout that could be used to make a few mortgage payments until you find work again.

- You might be in the kind of job where finding work is not too difficult and therefore MPPI is not so necessary.

- You might be in a position to re-arrange payments to your lender during the period that you are unable to work, perhaps by reducing them until then.

If you decide to buy, what should you be looking for?

As always, check every policy carefully to find one that's suitable for your circumstances. Below are the main points to watch for.

- Self-employed people and short-term contract workers sometimes find it hard to claim for unemployment. In the case of the self-employed, an insurer may only pay out if that person goes out of business, rather than simply being unable to get new work in.

- You will not be able to claim for any time off work due to an illness or disability that existed before you took out the policy.

- There is always a waiting period, usually ranging between 30 and 60 days before policies pay out when a claim is made.

- The policy will usually pay out for up to 12 months only, although some insurers offer longer benefit periods.

How much should you pay?

If you are buying cover from any lender, whether for a personal loan or a mortgage, expect to pay at least 60p to 70p a month for every £100 borrowed. So if you have borrowed £1,000 over one year, the PPI cover would add about £6 to £7 a month to your repayment costs. Or, when paying back £500 a month on a mortgage, MPPI can add up to £35 a month to repayments.

Part of the reason why mortgage protection in particular is so expensive is that there is always a problem of "adverse selection": people who think they might lose their jobs take out the cover and then claim, making it expensive for everyone else.

Wealth warning

Not only is PPI expensive, but many lenders add the full cost of the insurance itself to the loan at the outset, leaving customers to pay interest on the cover as well as the sum they borrow.

This is known as a single premium policy and is grotesquely expensive, costing policyholders up to 20 per cent of the cost of the loan over its lifetime. In a recent report, the Competition Commission watchdog said it wanted to see this kind of policy banned.

TOP TIP

Always get a quote from an independent insurer before you buy: they can be up to one third cheaper than your lender for the same cover.

Also, don't over-insure: if you already have good sickness benefits from your work, you don't need the sickness component of accident, sickness and unemployment (ASU) cover. It is possible to buy each component separately from a broker or an independent insurer.

Contacts and links

MoneyMadeClear: this is the Financial Services Authority's consumer information website. It includes advice on how to buy insurance and what questions to ask, as well as a jargon-buster. You can find more details here www.moneymadeclear.fsa.gov.uk

British Insurance Brokers Association (Biba): this is the trade body for brokers who specialise in selling general insurance. Its members are supposed to be experts in obtaining cover for all sorts of unusual insurance needs. It offers a postcode search system for a broker near you. That said, if you only need basic cover, you should be able to find it more cheaply from a price comparison website. Find it at www.biba.org.uk

Association of British Insurers: represents the insurance industry. Check it out at www.abi.org.uk

Get your own back

Every year hundreds of thousands of people who engage in some way with financial institutions of any and every variety will feel let down by the service they receive or the product they have bought.

It could be about anything: bank charges, an insurance policy that failed to pay out when it should have done, a mortgage company that took your money and then turned down your loan application, a financial adviser who recommended an 'ultra-safe' investment which plummeted 25 per cent in value overnight.

If it hasn't happened to you already, the odds are that it will at some stage.

In all such cases, it is easy to feel powerless and unable to do much about what has happened to you. After all, the forces ranged against you can seem pretty formidable.

The important thing to bear in mind is that, although not always totally effective, there is a wide range of mechanisms you can use to obtain redress from those you believe have wronged you. Even if you don't always win, at the very least you can make their life difficult, hopefully teaching them that they cannot treat you or others in the same way and hope to get away scot-free.

So what are the processes involved in complaining successfully against the financial giants? The striking fact is that regardless of whom you complain to later on, in almost every single case there is a common strategy to follow, certainly in the early stages.

Know what to complain about

Regardless of who or where you go to, you need to be sure what it is you are complaining about.

In almost every case, companies will have built up a raft of exclusions and small print designed to evade responsibility for what they have done – or failed to do. In other cases, even when you go to an official watchdog, you may be surprised to discover that they may not be able to accept jurisdiction.

For example, if you want to complain that your investment has plummeted in value by 30 per cent, you will probably be told that this is not an issue that can be addressed. But if you complain that your financial adviser told you this was a risk-free investment – and have a letter from the adviser saying so – you stand a far better chance of winning compensation.

So the first step is always to do lots of research into exactly what you feel are the key issues you want to complain about and why. Read the small print of any contract you have and work out ways of getting round any exclusions.

One of the best places to get more information in this area is the Financial Ombudsman Service. This is an industry-funded but impartial service which offers free advice and arbitration, dealing with tens of thousands of complaints a year.

More importantly in this context, its findings are binding on the industry and it has, over many years, built up a massive set of 'case law' that companies sometimes try to ignore but can be forced to obey. That kind of information is available either verbally from its advisers or on its website.

Who to complain to

In almost every instance, the first step is to go to the company itself.

Make sure you find out first exactly who you should be complaining to. Start with the person you originally dealt with. Get a name and title of someone to complain to, as well as their address. There's no point in scatter-gun correspondence all over the place.

That said, sometimes sending out copies of any correspondence to just about everyone up and down that individual's food chain can make both him/her and their superiors know that you are after their blood.

Always keep copies of all correspondence, record all phone calls, or keep notes of the conversation, plus details of who you are speaking to.

If you bought a policy through a broker or a financial adviser, they should be the people handling your complaint or your claim for you. But they may not always make that much effort on your behalf, so it is best to keep checking up on what and where they are up to.

Making a claim – what you need to know

So how can we make sure that we can get financial providers to meet legitimate claims? Let's look at the kind of things you would want to do for an insurance type of claim.

1 Check the policy before you buy

A lot of disputes happen because people think they are covered and discover too late that they are not. If that happens, complaining afterwards is not much use.

2 Utmost good faith

A contract between insured and insurer is based on the notion of 'utmost good faith'. This means you have a duty to disclose any information that may affect the granting of a policy, any exclusion that might be applied or its price.

Insurers also operate on the basis of: 'if in any doubt, tell us first'. Here, you are entitled to argue that in turning down your complaint the insurer would need to show that not being informed of a certain fact by you would have had a material impact on any eventual claim.

3 Keep records of what you are insuring

This may include a picture of the item at home, along with any purchase receipts or independent valuations.

4 Keep your valuables safe at all times

This is often defined by the Financial Ombudsman Service as a 'reasonable' duty of care. It means, for example, keeping valuables in the hotel safe or having the right amount of security in your home or car.

It may also mean taking precautions 'appropriate' to the item you are protecting. If you leave the keys of your Mercedes in the ignition as you go and pay for petrol at a service station, this will be treated differently than if you had done the same to an old, knackered Ford Fiesta.

5 Report all theft and loss swiftly

Make sure you obtain an incident report number from the police as proof that you have reported the loss.

6 Get your paperwork in order

Always follow your policy document to the letter. When you make any claim, provide all supporting documentation to back up what you say. Overwhelm them with suitable evidence, including receipts, photographs, copies of any police or medical reports you have.

You should always send copies to the insurer, not originals. But check first so as not to waste your time or theirs. If you do send any original documents, always make sure it is by recorded delivery.

Setting out your complaint

Don't become abusive or make threats that are impossible to keep. Instead, remain calm and try not to use words such as 'disgraceful', 'shoddy' or 'shocking'.

If you are seeking financial redress, ask for a reasonable amount for distress, but there's no point in demanding £1,000 for the time spent writing your eight-page letters. Explain why you want redress and, where possible, base it on actual monetary or financial loss suffered.

Once you have made a complaint

Financial services companies generally have eight weeks to give a final response to your complaint, unless they ask for a specific exemption from the financial watchdog, the Financial Services Authority.

If they do not reply within this time, or you are unhappy with their reply, you can go to the Financial Ombudsman Service.

Financial Ombudsman Service

The Financial Ombudsman Service (FOS) is the place to go if you have a financial complaint you cannot sort out with your insurance company, broker or financial adviser in respect of most financial products or services.

If it looks as if you cannot get the company to change its mind, you can ask for a 'failure to agree' or 'deadlock' letter and take the matter to the Financial Ombudsman Service.

- You have six months from the date of the final deadlock letter to complain to the Ombudsman.
- If your complaint can be dealt with, the Financial Ombudsman Service will usually start by seeing if it can help you and the company resolve matters informally, generally through mediation.
- Its staff will look at the facts and let you and the company know how they think you could reach agreement.
- If mediation is not an option, the Ombudsman then looks at the matter formally. Initially, an adjudicator will consider all the information and comments that you and the company have put forward, taking advice from the Ombudsman where appropriate.

The Ombudsman may also ask for documents and information from other people and companies linked to your case. So it may take some time before they can get to the bottom of your complaint.

The adjudicator will keep you up to date with progress on your case and will write to you to set out how your complaint should be resolved.

What happens after the Ombudsman's ruling?

Once an Ombudsman's decision is made on your case, it is final. Your insurance company has to accept the decision. But you don't. You are free to go to court instead.

If you decide to go down this route, the simplest way is to use a County Court, where there is a special procedure for smaller claims of £5,000 or less. The easiest place to go to is HM Courts Service's website; www.hmcourts-service.gov.uk. If your claim is for more than £5,000, you need to take legal advice.

Say you make a complaint and the Ombudsman finds in your favour. How much might you get? The maximum is £100,000, although the company you complain against may face a request by the FOS to make to a higher payment. Although it doesn't have to make it, most will do so. The payment is specifically in respect of financial losses suffered. But many people find that even when they win their claim with the FOS, it can be a legal nightmare, involving a number of letters. In such cases, the Ombudsman may also order payments for distress and inconvenience. This is defined in the following way by the FOS.

- 'Distress includes embarrassment, anxiety [and] disappointment. The degree of distress involved can vary widely: it can be little more than a relatively minor annoyance. In certain cases, however, it can cause worry, loss of sleep or even prolonged ill health.'

- 'Inconvenience can include any expenditure of time and/or effort by the customer that has resulted from the firm's conduct. Again, in relatively minor cases this may not amount to a significant burden. But it can include severe disruption and a great deal of wasted time.'

Payments for distress and inconvenience are normally around £50–£100 a day, and not more than £10 per hour. Most awards are for less than £300 and in only a small number of exceptional cases are they higher than £1,000. Awards involving pain and suffering are likely to be higher than those involving distress or inconvenience.

When a financial company goes belly-up

Being awarded compensation if something goes wrong is all well and good. But for many people in the past few months, the issue is less one of winning an argument with a financial provider, such as a bank or an insurer, but what happens if they go bust.

In such cases, the financial industry does have a fall-back 'fund of last resort' called the Financial Services Compensation Scheme, or FSCS, which is there to help. Its work, and the money it pays out, is paid for by a levy across the entire financial industry.

The aim, clearly, is to protect consumer confidence in the industry: were people to feel that they might not be compensated in the event of something going wrong, they would be far less likely to invest.

How the FSCS works

Let's create a scenario.

Say you were badly advised to take out a certain financial product. In front of witnesses, you specifically told your adviser that you wanted a safe haven for your money over a two-year period and he ignored your needs, placing your money into a very high-risk fund instead. You lost 50 per cent of your investment overnight.

By definition, this would be classed as a classic case of mis-selling and you would be almost certain to win a claim for compensation against that adviser, were you to make one to the Financial Ombudsman Service (FOS).

However, in most cases where something like this happens, it is highly unlikely to be an isolated instance; the adviser in question has probably been pulling the same stunt with other people, too.

In which case, he is likely to be facing not just one or two claims for compensation but several dozen, or even several hundred. He may also be under investigation by the Financial Services Authority (FSA), the leading financial watchdog, and publicity (even if only word-of-mouth) may well mean that more cases come out of the woodwork in light of any regulatory inquiry.

Under such circumstances, the likelihood of that adviser being able to afford to pay you compensation as determined by the FOS is slim to none. Even if he has a professional indemnity policy, something all advisers are required to have, it almost always has an 'excess' where he would have to pay the first few thousand pounds of any claim. Several claims will put paid to that.

He will simply go bust, declaring himself insolvent.

The cavalry arrives

This is where the FSCS comes in. It acts when a firm has been declared to be 'in default', which basically mean that as a result of financial circumstances such as insolvency, for example, it is unable to meet a claim for compensation.

In addition to the scenario above, the FSCS might also act in situations where a firm collapses suddenly, for example an insurer with hundreds of thousands of car policies, or – as we saw at the end of 2008 – when many tens of thousands of investors lost money they had placed in accounts with a number of Icelandic banks. Here, the FSCS was the organisation which arranged for those affected to receive compensation.

Who is covered by the FSCS

Broadly speaking, there are a number of financial providers where the FSCS is able to help people seeking compensation. Its remit is over:

- UK banks authorised by the FSA, including their branches in the European Economic Area (EEA);
- EEA banks if they have joined the UK scheme in order to top up the cover available from their home state compensation scheme for deposits taken by their UK branches;
- non-EEA banks for deposits taken by their UK branches;
- building societies in the UK;
- credit unions (but not in Northern Ireland).

However, the FSCS can only pay out if the activities that the firm in question engaged in were regulated by the Financial Services Authority. This means that financial schemes operating outside the UK may not be protected.

The Icelandic case above involved UK-authorised subsidiaries of Icelandic banks, which allowed compensation to be paid. But several thousand policyholders whose money was held in separate accounts by an Isle of Man subsidiary were not covered. Nor would they have been if their bank was based in the Channel Islands.

There are three main product areas where you might be able to get compensation.

- **Life and general insurance contracts.** This covers anything from life insurance to home and contents cover. Note that the word 'insurance' also covers many investment-type products, such as endowments and even some pensions.

The FSCS will try to safeguard policyholders, for example by arranging for their policies to be transferred to another firm. If this is not possible, it will arrange for compensation to be paid to them so that they can take out another policy.

■ **Investments.** This applies if you suffer losses as a result of bad investment advice, negligent investment management or misrepresentation, or if an 'authorised' investment firm goes out of business and cannot return your investments or money owed to you. Investments covered include stocks and shares, unit trusts, futures and options, personal pension plans and other long-term policies.

By the way, please note the word 'authorised': a payout won't be made if you lost money because you were contacted by some scammer in, say, Nigeria and innocently handed him your entire inheritance. It is your responsibility to check first that the firm you are doing business with is authorised by the Financial Services Authority to engage in that activity. Almost always, a simple call would tell you that.

■ **Mortgages.** Since the end of 2004, if you took out a home-related loan (such as a mortgage) based on advice which was unsuitable for you and you lost money as a result, you might be able to make a claim – assuming the firm goes bust.

An example might be if, say, you went to a mortgage broker and explained that as someone who was self-employed you needed a mortgage with the option of making flexible payments to take into account your varying income. He placed you into an unsuitable five-year fixed deal with a very rigid payment structure – and expensive penalties for cancelling the contract.

The compensation process

Deciding whether a firm is in default is a decision taken either by the FSCS itself or by the watchdog it works alongside, the FSA. If this turns out to be the case, the FSCS will invite investors or policyholders who have previously not come forward to contact its staff and make a claim if they feel they are entitled to one.

Assuming it has the firm's records, it will write to everyone concerned, as well as issue media releases to generate more publicity.

When you write in, you will be sent a form to claim and asked to provide any supporting information to help the FSCS decide your claim. It aims to settle all claims in respect of a firm in default within six months.

How much you might get

Unfortunately, there are limits on how much can be paid. The first point to note is that you will only be offered compensation for actual losses suffered, not for distress or inconvenience. The amount paid will try to put you back in the position you would have been in if you had not invested.

The amounts available vary depending on which product you have. This is a by-product of the fact that the FSCS is a cobbled-together organisation which used to consist of smaller schemes, each specific to their individual financial area.

Inevitably, there are also minor wrinkles in terms of eligibility, exactly who can receive what and so on. But the basic rules are as follows.

■ Deposits, such as bank or savings accounts – up to £50,000 per person is covered, with 100 per cent of that sum being paid.

- Insurance – the first £2,000 of an insurance claim or policy is covered in full, plus 90 per cent of the balance. Claims about so-called 'compulsory' insurance, such as car-related policies, are covered in full.
- Investments – up to £48,000 (100 per cent of £30,000 and 90 per cent of the next £20,000).
- Home finance, for example mortgage advice and arranging a mortgage – up to £48,000 (100 per cent of £30,000 and 90 per cent of the next £20,000).

If you have a compensation claim to make, the FSCS can be contacted on: 020 7892 7300. Its website address is: www.fscs.org.uk

Contacts and links

Financial Services Authority: the City's leading financial watchdog can be found at www.fsa.gov.uk

Office of Fair Trading: enforces consumer protection law and competition law. It can be found at www.oft.gov.uk

Financial Ombudsman Service: where to go if you have a complaint about a financial provider or an adviser. Find it at www.financial-ombudsman.org.uk or call 0845 080 1800.

Index